Sports and Technology Have the Power to Change the World

Driving Positive Change Through the Use of Data and AI

Jon Flynn

WILEY

To the loves of my life, Bernadette, Sadie, and Avery.

Contents

Foreword

In 2009, I worked as a sports industry journalist in London. The 2012 Olympic and Paralympic Games were on the horizon, and the British capital felt like it was at the center of the sporting world. As a result, with so many eyes on the city and so many high-level sports conferences calling it home, it became a regular stopping point for delegations from the countries bidding to host the 2018 and 2022 FIFA World Cups. Equipped with well-designed decks, scale-model stadiums, slick presentations, and multimillion-dollar budgets, 11 bidding teams from 13 countries sought to convince the media and the world that they would represent the best hosts for the global game's most-watched tournament.

There were more talking points than could fit in this book, let alone the foreword. Among them all, though, I remember being repeatedly amazed by the Japanese bid. Never among the frontrunners, and perhaps because it had co-hosted the tournament as recently as 2002, it was the bid that felt most focused on the future: Japan pledged the development of technology that would allow hundreds of stadiums around the world to show the games in real-time 3D coverage and via holographic projection; second screens would allow the instant sharing of groundbreaking data; augmented reality (AR) and virtual reality (VR) were key to every element of the fan experience; microphones would be embedded in innovative locations to capture sounds never heard before by viewers at home; and translation earpieces would let fans from around the world cross-linguistic divides.

It was science fiction, and reality won out in every sense. The bidding process ended up mired in controversy, with multiple members of the voting committee ultimately arrested and banned from the sport. The stories of corruption continued past the hosting of the events themselves a decade and more later.

In the meantime, I moved on from writing about the business of sport to working in it and then to its role in changing the world—helping to scale and lead the Laureus Sport for Good Foundation, founded under the Patronage of Nelson Mandela and charged with using sport to end violence, discrimination, and inequality. Along the way, I met Jon Flynn, a man who shares the belief in the power of sport to have a positive impact on the world but who is also relentlessly committed to helping it innovate as a sector. In this book, he tells the story of Erik Spoelstra and Dwyane Wade at the Miami Heat, talking of Spoelstra "instilling in Wade the mindset of continuous improvement"—a mindset Jon certainly shares in his own work with many of the biggest organizations in the sporting world and which sums up the technological advances in the sports business over the intervening period (not that every traditionalist welcomes some of the resulting changes).

By as early as 2014, as Jon says in his analysis of the science behind the German men's team's march to the 2014 World Cup trophy, technology had become "a defining narrative that reshaped the game and enriched the fan experience." Premier League fans frustrated with the current implementation of the video assistant referee (VAR) might take umbrage at that last point, but it remains the case, and for more than the experience on the pitch or for those watching on television. The worlds of technology and social impact collide in the literal arena of sport—forget VAR, forget player data or sports science, and think of a simple example cited in these pages. By 2018, all FIFA's digital platforms were designed to be compatible with screen readers and featured closed captioning; by 2022, in fact, and for all the challenges and criticisms of that tournament, the stadiums in Qatar became the first to feature "sensory rooms" as a place of refuge for children and young adults with autism. Augmented reality was woven into the experience of the tournament, and as a result, consumption of the world's most popular sport reached new audiences and broke down new barriers, while fans reveled in the use of Google Translate and other tools to communicate with those who spoke other languages. Much of the science fiction of the Japanese bid had become reality.

Meanwhile, between the delivery of those eventual tournaments in 2018 and 2022, the FIFA Women's World Cup in France in 2019 saw the players of the U.S. women's national team (USWNT) use technology in their own way, driving the #EqualPay campaign via social media. As Jon covers in this book, this was not just about the reach of their tweets or a memorable hashtag. The analytics, the understanding of how the message was landing, and the resulting subtle adjustments to the tenor of communications, let the USWNT players really drive their fight for gender equity. They would go on to land compensation from their own governing body and a new pay deal in which they split World Cup prize money equally with the men's team. Without technology, the fight that took many years would have taken even longer.

Sport is the great equalizer, the great meritocracy. We love it for that. When done properly, as President Mandela said, "Sport has the power to change the world." Yes, it can get so much wrong: it can be exclusionary rather than inclusive; it can sideline those who don't fit the mold or are unable to access the best opportunities; corruption and sportswashing can raise globally challenging questions. The same is true of technology, but despite the challenges, when it is done properly and with the right goals in mind, its positive impacts are often inarguable. Whether in the world of sports or the world of technology, neither happens without intention—but both can make the world a better place. And together, they really can have an impact.

Adam Fraser

Adam Fraser is the former chief executive of the Laureus Sport for Good Foundation, which has raised more than $200 million and impacted the lives of almost seven million children around the world. He is currently the CEO of Terraset, a nonprofit using philanthropic capital to catalyze the nascent carbon removal industry and tackle climate change. After all, without a planet, we don't have anywhere to play sport.

Introduction

Throughout human history, few things have been as consistently vibrant, universally impactful, and profoundly unifying as the world of sports. From the ancient Olympic Games of Greece to the modern-day spectacle of the FIFA World Cup or the Superbowl, sports have always held an unequaled power to bring people together; to transcend cultural, racial, and political divides; and to inspire a collective sense of purpose and camaraderie. This book seeks to dive deeper into the transformative power of sports and how they have been and continue to be, a potent catalyst for positive change.

In the following chapters, I will explore the myriad ways in which sports have been instrumental in breaking down barriers, both physical and metaphorical, and in driving social progress. I will delve into the stories of individuals, teams, and nations who have used sports platform challenge norms, fight for justice, and bring about significant societal change across multiple and lasting dimensions.

However, the narrative of sports as a force for good is is about more than just the athletes and the games they play. It is also about the critical role that technology has played in amplifying the ability of athletes to excel in their sport and the impact of sports around the world. From the advent of broadcast technology that brought games into our living rooms to the rise of social media that has connected fans across the globe, technology has fundamentally reshaped the landscape of sports. It has made sports more accessible, more engaging, and more influential than ever before. Thanks to technology, the reach of sports is truly global and has become a platform on which change can be built and delivered.

In this book, I will also highlight how technology has been harnessed to enhance the power of sports to effect positive change. I will look at how data analytics has revolutionized player performance and team strategies, how virtual and augmented reality is used to make sports more inclusive, and how digital platforms enable athletes to amplify their voices on important social issues.

Furthermore, I will explore the role of diplomacy in sports, examining how sporting events have served as platforms for diplomatic engagement and conflict resolution. From the ping-pong diplomacy of the 1970s to the more recent instances of sports diplomacy in the Korean Peninsula, I will delve into the ways in which sports have been used as a tool for fostering understanding and promoting peace as the ultimate universal language and great equalizer for everyone on the planet.

Through these narratives, this book aims to comprehensively explore the power of sports, technology, and diplomacy to drive positive change. By examining these specific cases, my aim to inspire a deeper appreciation of the potential of sports, not just as a source of entertainment but as a powerful force for good in the world. So, let us embark on this journey together, exploring the transformative power of sports and the endless possibilities they hold for shaping a better future.

The Impact of Advanced Data Analytics

2013 NBA Finals: Miami Heat vs. San Antonio Spurs

In 2013, tensions were high as the Miami Heat and San Antonio Spurs squared off for Game 1 of the NBA Finals. The energy in Miami, a town known for its love of basketball, was high. The fans were ready and came out in droves to support their teams, breaking attendance records to rally behind their beloved teams. The two Titans had met in the Finals just two years earlier, with the Heat coming out on top in a thrilling seven-game series. The echoes of past showdowns between these two titans resonated in the air, leaving basketball aficionados craving more of the heart-stopping drama they witnessed just a short two years earlier. This time, however, there was an added element of competition. Both the Heat and the Spurs had embraced the cutting-edge advancements of advanced data analytics and video technology at their disposal, and both teams were better prepared than ever before. Each side was armed with a team of extremely skilled data analysts in addition to their quota of coaching staff. These data analysts provided important insights to the coaching staff on decisions that could mean the difference between deploying a reverse layup or a power layup. The data provided by the analysts affected the starting lineup and substitutions during the game. These advanced data analytics could mean the difference between a win and a loss. Every decision mattered, and the information provided by these analysts became the tactical ammunition that could tip the scales in their favor. These types of analytics had never been so widely used and relied upon in any NBA Finals game before. Clearly, the teams that adopted a data-driven decision-making strategy were creating their own off-court advantage.

In the locker room before the game, Miami Heat coach Erik Spoelstra and his team of analysts poured over data on the Spurs' offensive and defensive strategies, looking for weaknesses to exploit. They had spent months studying data covering every aspect of the Spurs' game, from their pick-and-roll strategies to their transition defense. Coach Spoelstra was no stranger to using data and analytics to create insights that gained ground against opponents. In fact, the Heat's coach was first hired as the team's video coordinator in 1995. The role of a video coordinator in basketball is crucial to a team's success. The video coordinator is responsible for managing and analyzing game footage and other video resources to provide valuable insights to the coaching staff and players. Their primary objective is to enhance team performance through the strategic use of video analysis. The video coordinator utilizes specialized software and technology to break down game footage and extract meaningful information. They employ video-editing tools to create customized playlists, highlight reels, and scouting reports. They use tagging systems to label specific plays, player actions, and other relevant events, allowing quick retrieval and analysis. This enables the coaching staff to focus on specific aspects of the game, such as offensive and defensive sets, player tendencies, and opponent strategies. Spoelstra spent two seasons in that role before moving up to assistant coach/video coordinator. He was promoted to assistant coach/advance scout in 1999 and became the Heat's assistant coach/director of scouting in 2001. The time he spent pouring over videos, analyzing every aspect of the Heat's and opponents' games, provided the perfect training ground for his impact when the time came for him to take the reins as head coach of the Heat.

This experience and discipline in examining players' data from video footage are widely attributed to the great work Spoelstra did with Dwayne Wade and the impact he had on his career. He recognized Wade's strengths (such as his explosive athleticism, scoring ability, and basketball IQ) and designed offensive sets and strategies that maximized Wade's impact. Spoelstra emphasized playing to Wade's strengths, creating opportunities for him to excel in driving to the basket, utilizing his midrange game, and making decisive plays in transition. By tailoring the team's offensive system to Wade's abilities, Spoelstra allowed him to showcase his skills and significantly impact the game.

Coach Spoelstra worked closely with Wade to refine his overall game. He provided guidance and mentorship to help Wade improve his shooting mechanics, decision-making, and defensive skills. Spoelstra emphasized the importance of discipline, work ethic, and attention to detail, instilling the continuous movement mindset in Wade. Under Spoelstra's guidance, Wade honed his skills, developed a versatile offensive repertoire, and became a more complete player.

Coach Spoelstra's strategic acumen and ability to make in-game adjustments were instrumental in Wade's and the team's success. He recognized the importance of putting players in positions to succeed and made timely substitutions and strategic moves to optimize the team's performance. Spoelstra's ability to analyze game situations, devise effective game plans, and adapt to changing circumstances created an environment where players such as Wade could thrive. Thanks to his time in the video coordinator role, Spoelstra was uniquely positioned to see the bigger picture and identify insights through the help of data analysis. His years of breaking down game footage helped set his team up for success, no matter what their opponents brought to the court.

Meanwhile, San Antonio Spurs coach Gregg Popovich was doing the same, using advanced analytics to identify the Heat's strengths and weaknesses. He had a team of highly skilled, highly motivated analysts who were constantly crunching numbers and analyzing video footage, looking for ways to gain an edge over their opponents. It was here that the amount of, and most importantly, the quality of the data meant the difference between a right or wrong call. Coach Pop, as he is affectionally known, once said, "I look at the analytics. Some of it is very worthwhile. Some of it is superfluous poppycock." His ability to separate the worthwhile analytics from the not-so-worthwhile was a valuable skill in 2013. The advancements made since 2013 have helped Pop eliminate most of the "poppycock" from the analysis before it makes its way to the coaching staff!

Coach Pop is beloved in San Antonio and beyond for his skills as a basketball coach. In fact, as of the 2023 season, Popovich was the winningest NBA head coach of all time, with 1,364 wins under his belt. His coaching style has been instrumental in the success and development of players on the San Antonio Spurs. Known for his unique approach, Pop created a culture of excellence, teamwork, and selflessness within the Spurs organization. His coaching style emphasized certain key aspects that greatly benefited the players.

First and foremost, Popovich prioritized building strong relationships with his players. He genuinely cared about their well-being and took the time to understand their individual strengths, weaknesses, and motivations. By establishing trust and fostering open communication, he created an environment where players felt comfortable expressing themselves and seeking guidance to help with all aspects of their lives, on and off the court. This approach allowed Popovich to connect with his players on a personal level, which in turn enhanced their commitment and dedication to the team. His coaching style involved adapting strategies and game plans to maximize his players' strengths. He tailored the team's offensive and defensive systems to fit the skills and abilities of his roster. Popovich emphasized a cohesive and selfless playing style characterized by ball movement, unselfishness, and high basketball IQ. This approach allowed players to showcase their abilities while also creating opportunities for their teammates to excel. Popovich's strategic acumen and willingness to adjust tactics based on the strengths and weaknesses of the team contributed to the Spurs' success. His comments on analytics notwithstanding, his ability to quickly take action based on the data his team of coaches and highly skilled analysts provided him proved to be a deadly combination on the court.

Many players on the Spurs' roster experienced development under Popovich's coaching during the 2013 season, such as Tony Parker, Tim Duncan, and Manu Ginobili. However, the growth and emergence of Kawhi Leonard as a force on both ends of the court made him one of the most notable success stories of that season. Popovich recognized Leonard's immense potential and played a pivotal role in his development as a versatile two-way player.

On the defensive end, Popovich entrusted Leonard with the task of guarding some of the league's most formidable players. Through intense practices and individual coaching, Popovich helped Leonard refine his defensive skills, positioning, and understanding of defensive schemes. Leonard's defensive prowess flourished under Popovich's guidance, as he became known for his ability to shut down opponents and make crucial steals and deflections.

Offensively, Popovich worked with Leonard to expand his skill set and confidence. Popovich's offensive system emphasized ball movement and player motion, and he encouraged Leonard to take on a more significant offensive role. Popovich instilled in Leonard the importance of efficiency, shot selection, and decision-making. As a result, Leonard's offensive game grew, and he became a reliable scorer, capable of attacking the rim, knocking down midrange jumpers, and even developing a three-point shot.

As the Finals began, it quickly became clear that both coaches and both teams were incredibly well-versed in their opponent's style of play and were able to quickly identify and exploit any weakness or misstep made. This set the tone for the grueling battle between two teams that both wanted to win, both wanted that trophy and bragging rights, and both were prepared to give it their all to do so. The series went all the way, with the teams meeting in game 7, having won 3 games each, to battle one last time in a do-or-die final. Ultimately, the Heat prevailed 95 to 88 in game 7 and were crowned the 2013 NBA Season Champions. Their win is thanks in part to the massive talent they had on their roster: LeBron James, Dwayne Wade, and Chris Bosch were simply outstanding, and LeBron James was named NBA Finals MVP, thanks in part to the data-rich technologies they used as part of their strategy. Miami Heat's ultimate four games to-three victory in the 2013 NBA Finals made everyone realize the importance of advanced data analytics and video technology in sports.

On the heels of their victory, Miami Heat players basked in the glory of their success while reflecting on the hard work and dedication that led them to the championship. The Heat knew they could not have achieved this feat without using advanced data analytics and video technology that was so expertly deployed during the seven-game Finals. Throughout the series, the Heat harnessed the power of advanced data analytics to gain a competitive edge. The team leveraged sophisticated statistical models and player-tracking data to uncover hidden patterns and insights. By analyzing vast amounts of data, they were able to identify the most effective offensive plays, defensive strategies, and lineup combinations. This data-driven approach enabled the coaching staff to make informed decisions based on concrete evidence rather than mere intuition or conventional wisdom.

Furthermore, they embraced the use of video technology as a critical tool in their game planning and preparation. They meticulously studied game footage, scrutinizing every aspect of their own performance and that of their opponents. Through the use of video analysis software, the Heat coaching staff dissected offensive and defensive schemes, player tendencies, and tactical intricacies. This in-depth analysis allowed them to devise tailored game plans, exploit weaknesses in the opposing team's defense, and adjust their real-time strategies based on the unfolding dynamics of each game.

LeBron James was particularly grateful for the data-driven approach. In the post-game interview, he said, "We knew what we had to do. We knew how the Spurs would play us, and we were ready for it. It's all thanks to the analytics team we have and the technology that we use to study our opponents." The Heat's coach, Erik Spoelstra, was also quick to credit the team's success to using advanced data analytics. He noted that the Heat used advanced data analytics to study the Spurs' offensive and defensive strategies and were able to identify patterns and exploit their weaknesses. Using this technology, they were able to adjust their game plan dynamically and maximize the players' strengths against the Spurs.

The San Antonio Spurs also recognized the immense value of data and technology in their pursuit of victory. The team employed advanced data analytics to gain insights into player performance, team efficiency, and strategic decision-making. The Spurs used statistical models and algorithms to evaluate lineups, optimize rotations, and analyze the effectiveness of various offensive and defensive strategies. By leveraging the power of data-driven insights, the coaching staff was able to make informed adjustments, exploit matchup advantages, and maximize the contributions of each player.

Video technology also played a pivotal role for the San Antonio Spurs. They meticulously analyzed game footage and employed video tracking systems to gain a comprehensive understanding of their opponents' playing style and tendencies. This allowed them to identify patterns, anticipate plays, and devise defensive schemes to neutralize the strengths of their opponents. Video technology not only aided in scouting and game planning but also served as a valuable tool for player development. The Spurs utilized video analysis to provide personalized feedback to players, identify areas for improvement, and refine their skills and techniques.

It is clear that the use of technology played a significant role in the 2013 NBA Finals. For both teams, technology was heavily used for player performance tracking, scouting, and strategic planning. One significant piece of technology used was SportVU from Stats Perform, a sports data company. SportVU is a camera-based system that was installed in all NBA arenas that captured the positional data of players and the ball 25 times per second. This data could be analyzed to provide detailed insights about player movement, shooting efficiency, defensive effectiveness, and other aspects of the game in real time. Teams could use this real-time data to make dynamic adjustments in their game plans and player rotations throughout the 2013 NBA Finals. Having this rich data available to their team of analysts, they could create sophisticated models that crunched the data at speeds far outpacing those possible by humans. This allowed the results to be returned in almost real-time fashion once the data was fed into the models. It played a significant role for both teams in the coaching staff's ability to make data-drive decisions around their strategies for each game and the incredibly detailed information the data was telling them. For example, the starting lineup could be changed on the fly once the opposing team's lineup was announced; substitutions could be made based on opposing team moves, score, time left in the quarter, strategy shift to defensive or offensive priority in real time. This ability inserted a level of predictive analytics that helped the coaching staff anticipate and answer moves made by their opposition with greater confidence.

The use of video analysis software was also a game-changer in the 2013 NBA Finals, with both teams using this technology to study their performance as well as their opponents'. This video analysis software from Catapult allowed them to identify patterns, weaknesses, and opportunities that could be exploited in future games. This gave the analyst teams data on each athlete on the court, which Catapult calls the Basketball Movement Profile. This profile provides data-driven insights into an athlete's movements, workload, stress, etc. These data points are then synchronized to the video footage. This type of technology has become a standard practice across the NBA, with teams employing dedicated video coordinators and analysts to manage and interpret the data. The ability for the teams to make use of near real-time video analytics through the use of the Catapult technology allowed them to review plays and analyze player performance easily. Coupling this data with the game strategy and decisions, the coaching staff was able to quickly identify which decisions were effective and which were less effective. Catapult's technology was also able to provide a live halftime capture capability. This feature enabled teams to review insights at halftime, thus allowing them to make any needed adjustments prior to the second half. Having the ability to tap into this level of data using a tablet on the sideline was a major advancement in the data-driven decision-making tools that assist coaches. Both the Miami Heat and the San Antonio Spurs used the data derived from Catapult to much success through the 2013 NBA Finals, and they still make use of video analysis tools today—although the advancements in this technology from 2013 to today have been tremendous, and the pace of innovation is increasing.

One of the major advancements in video analysis software has been thanks to the rise of cloud computing. Cloud computing has removed storage limits, allowing for full-time recording and easy access to past games and clips. This technology made it possible for teams to set up shortcuts to in-game clipping, show players clips from previous games or seasons to help them work on specific areas of their game, and allow coaches to scout players and patterns of teams early. This allows more sophisticated data models to be created using the video analysis data to strengthen a data-driven decision that the model makes. In the broader context of sports data analysis, video analysis tools offer significant advantages. They allow for the tracking and visualization of play patterns, aiding in decision-making during a game. They can also be used for training purposes, helping coaching staff and athletes identify areas of weaknesses and strengths at the individual athlete and team levels.

Advanced analytics have existed long before Coach Spoelstra and Coach Popovich faced each other in the 2013 NBA Finals. The first widely reported use of statistics in a 1938 basketball game, when Coach Howard Hobson led Oregon to its first NCAA championship. He has credited analyzing the game of basketball through statistics as a major influence on his coaching style. He published a book in 1949 called *Scientific Basketball*. We have Coach Hobson to thank for the widening of the free-throw line and the introduction and implementation of the shot clock as well as the 3-point line.

In the mid-1950s, Coach Dean Smith, inducted into the Hall of Fame after a 36-year run at North Carolina, where he coached the GOAT, Michael Jordan, created an evaluation system that measured the team's offensive and defensive efficacy via a possession metric. He felt that the current analysis that only included box score and total points scored failed to take possession or pace into account. Coach Smith revolutionized the game of basketball with his analytical approach, particularly through the introduction of the Four Corners offense. This innovative offensive system emphasized precise decision-making, exploiting defensive vulnerabilities and controlling the tempo of the game.

The Four Corners offense was a disciplined and patient strategy that aimed to create scoring opportunities through deliberate ball movement, spacing, and constant player motion. Coach Smith's analytical mindset was evident in his emphasis on exploiting matchups and capitalizing on defensive weaknesses. By spending time to document, review, and analyze his opponents' defensive tendencies, he strategically positioned his players to exploit vulnerabilities and create scoring opportunities. A key analytical component of the Four Corners offense was its ability to control the game's tempo. Coach Smith recognized the value of managing the clock and dictating the pace of play. By slowing down the game, his teams limited opponents' possessions, minimized scoring opportunities, and maintained a competitive edge against more talented opponents.

This approach was completely unique at the time, and the results had an incredible impact on the performance of the North Carolina basketball team. Coach Smith compiled a remarkable overall record of 879 wins and 254 losses. This impressive winning percentage of approximately 77 percent solidified his status as one of the most successful coaches in college basketball history. His teams won a total of 17 Atlantic Coast Conference regular-season championships and 13 Atlantic Coast Conference Tournament championships. Coach Smith guided the Tar Heels to 11 Final Four appearances and two national championships, capturing the NCAA title in 1982 and 1993.

The analytical revolution ignited by Coach Smith's Four Corners offense paved the way for a greater integration of data and technology in basketball. His emphasis on precise decision-making, exploiting defensive weaknesses, and controlling tempo demonstrated the transformative power of analytics. The impact of his analytical contributions extends beyond his teams at North Carolina, shaping the modern game of basketball and emphasizing the ongoing role of analytics in maximizing performance and achieving success. In today's game, analytics continue to play a crucial role. The evolution of technology and data analysis has provided coaches and teams with a wealth of information to inform their strategies. Advanced statistical models, player tracking data, and video analysis have become invaluable tools in understanding player performance, identifying tendencies, and optimizing offensive and defensive systems.

Data, and the practice of performing analysis on this data, has always been central to the game of basketball, to any sport for that matter. These early journeys into the world of statistics, mathematical probabilities, and measurement created the way for the Godfather of Sabermetrics, Bill James, to expand on these methodologies through data analysis for the game of baseball. This became known as *moneyball* and became immensely popular throughout all sports and in Hollywood thanks to Brad Pitt and Jonah Hill starring in the 2011 blockbuster *Moneyball*.

Inspired by the work and results that James' Sabermetrics was producing, statistician Lawrence Dean Oliver sought to apply this to the game of basketball. In 2004 he penned the book *Basketball on Paper: Rules and Tools for Performance Analysis*, which is widely regarded as the most influential book on data analytics of its time and led to the wide adoption of advanced data analytics as standard practice within basketball. Today, advanced data analytics not only lead to insights that help win games through affecting in-game decision-making but are also used off the court when it comes to trade decisions, draft analysis, training regimes, coaching matchups, player matchups, and helping players stay healthier and enjoy longer careers.

The impact of the 2013 NBA Finals extended far beyond the realm of the basketball court. It served as a catalyst for the widespread adoption and advancement of data analytics in basketball and sports as a whole. The victory of the Miami Heat and the recognition of the importance of advanced analytics in their success validated the use of innovative technologies in maximizing athlete and team performance. Following the 2013 NBA Finals, the sports world witnessed a surge in the use of data analytics across various sports disciplines. The success of the Miami Heat showcased the immense value of leveraging advanced statistical models, player tracking data, and video analysis to gain a competitive edge. This realization led teams across different leagues and sports to invest heavily in data analytics and technology, employing dedicated analytics departments and hiring experts in the field.

Moreover, the impact of the 2013 NBA Finals extended beyond professional sports organizations. The availability of sports data and analytics tools to fans has revolutionized the way enthusiasts engage with the game. Through the Internet and mobile devices, coupled with easy access to data, fans can access a wealth of statistics, create sophisticated models, and analyze the game in ways that were once limited to professional analysts. The access to, and influence of, advanced data analytics has brought fans closer to the game they love, enabling them to delve into the intricacies of basketball strategy, player performance, and team dynamics. Several NBA teams have implemented a second-screen experience through a phone or tablet app, providing fans with an interactive data-driven experience that coincides with the televised or streamed game. This creates a dynamic atmosphere and fuels a deeply personal engagement experience throughout the fan journey, allowing them to engage with the on-screen action.

The influence of data analytics on basketball continues to evolve and innovate with each passing season. As technology advances, new sources of data become available, and analytics techniques become more sophisticated. The basketball community continually seeks novel ways to leverage data and technology to gain a competitive advantage and enhance the overall fan experience. From the development of advanced player tracking systems to the use of artificial intelligence and machine learning algorithms, data analytics has become an integral part of the modern basketball landscape. If you were to take a look at the makeup of a basketball team today, you would find just as many, if not more, data engineers and analysts as you would coaching staff that help propel their teams and athletes to the top of their game. The impact of the 2013 NBA Finals on the world of data analytics in basketball has been transformative.

It has fueled a furious pace of innovation, pushing the boundaries of what's possible both on and off the court. Countless start-ups have emerged, offering keen insights into all aspects of the game and even inventing new areas to measure, examine, and create competitive advantage. As teams and fans embrace data analytics, the game continues to evolve, strategies adapt, and new insights are uncovered. The marriage of data analytics and basketball has created a dynamic synergy that propels the sport to new heights and captivates fans around the globe.

The 2013 NBA Finals stands as a landmark event in showcasing the potential use of data analytics in basketball to impact game strategy and execution of that strategy based on real-time insights. Its effects are demonstrable in multiple areas of basketball, inspiring further growth, boosting player capabilities, and bringing the game closer to all its fans. The progress of advanced data analytics in basketball exhibits just how influential technology can be and the desire for greatness that lies within sports analytics. In Coach Spoelstra's words, "Sometimes, you have a hunch, and then you find numbers that confirm it, making everyone—staff or players—say, 'Okay, let's fix that.'"

2

Using Sports Science to Optimize Player Performance

2014 FIFA World Cup: Germany's Victory

The Maracanã Stadium in Rio de Janeiro was alive! More than a billion people across the world tuned in, captivated by the beautiful game. It was July 13, 2014, and the sun was setting on a day that had been etched into the calendars of football fans across the globe for years. Inside the stadium, the air was thick with the electricity of 100,000 dreams, each one pinned on the 22 men who would soon take to the pitch. This was the 2014 FIFA World Cup final, the pinnacle of the footballing world, and they were the gladiators about to enter into battle.

The stadium was a sea of color, a vibrant tapestry woven from the flags of two proud footballing nations. The German black, red, and gold clashed spectacularly with Argentina's blue and white stripes, creating a spectacle that was as mesmerizing as the match that was about to begin. The fans, their faces painted, their voices rising in unison, created an atmosphere that was nothing short of intoxicating. On the pitch, the players were the picture of focused intensity. Their faces were masks of concentration; their bodies coiled springs of potential energy. They were acutely aware of the magnitude of the occasion, what brought them here in this moment, and the reality of a "winner takes all" match.

Both teams were ready to bring the trophy home with them and enjoy the spoils of victory.

The referee's whistle brought an already charged atmosphere to an electrifying peak and the game began. The ball moved quickly from one player to the next as the world's greatest footballers displayed their best skills. The German side was a perfectly synchronized machine, while the Argentinians played with a combination of raw talent and emotion. The contest looked like a chess match in its complexity and speed, a captivating display of tactics and technique. In the first half, there were plenty of close calls on both sides, but neither team could manage to score. Manuel Neuer, Germany's goalkeeper, was a dominant force between the posts. Lionel Messi, arguably the beautiful game's greatest player, dazzled with his quick footwork for Argentina, yet neither was able to break through the defense. As the match progressed, tensions mounted, and the crowd roared every move made by either team. Both players and fans alike were worn out from excitement and exertion. All eyes were fixed on the prize—just one goal away from victory.

And then, in the 113th minute, it happened. André Schürrle, the German forward, sent a cross into the box, and the midfielder, Mario Götze, controlled the ball with an effortless touch before perfectly targeting it into the back of the net. The crowd at Maracanã erupted in cheers; German fans roared with a wave of jubilation and relief as their players swarmed Götze in celebration of their inevitable victory.

The final whistle blew, and thunderous applause filled the stadium that could be heard around the world. The German team, their faces containing a mix of exhaustion and joy, embraced each other after achieving the outcome they had traveled to Brazil for. They had done it—they were champions of the world.

The 2014 FIFA World Cup left no doubt that sports science was the critical component of top-level teams. Football athlete performances were analyzed using GPS tracking and data from video recordings rather than actual game results. The goal of each team in using these newfound technologies and data science capabilities was to be able to predict opposing players' moves and counter with their own moves with perfect accuracy. It worked. The champions played like a well-oiled machine, dominating their opponents in all aspects of the game.

How did Germany get here? How did they become the champions of the world in 2014? Let's take a look at how the German Football Association (DFB), the governing body responsible for the German national team, used sports science as their secret weapon during the

FIFA 2014 World Cup. Many of the techniques used by the winning squad have been widely adopted across global football and see continuous innovation today.

First, let's take a quick look at how the FIFA World Cup, the biggest international football tournament, works and is responsible for bringing together teams from FIFA's member associations to crown the best of the best. The 2014 FIFA World Cup, like other editions of the tournament, followed a specific structure in terms of competition, team selection, and the number of games:

- **Qualification:** Before the main tournament, teams have to go through a qualification process in their respective continental zones, organized by their respective confederations (AFC for Asia, CAF for Africa, CONCACAF for North and Central America and the Caribbean, CONMEBOL for South America, OFC for Oceania, and UEFA for Europe). The number of spots each confederation gets in the World Cup is determined by FIFA.

- **Tournament structure:** As of 2014, the World Cup tournament involves 32 teams (this is set to expand to 48 teams in 2026). The teams are divided into eight groups of four (groups A to H). This stage is known as the *group stage*.

- **Group stage:** In the group stage, each team plays three matches, one against each of the other teams in their group. The matches are played in a round-robin format. Teams receive three points for a win, one for a draw, and no points for a loss. The top two teams from each group, based on points and then goal difference if points are equal, advance to the next stage, known as the *knockout stage* or *round of 16*.

- **Knockout stage:** From this point on, the tournament is a single-elimination competition. The teams play one match against their opponent, and the winner advances to the next round. In the event of a draw after 90 minutes, the match goes into extra time (two periods of 15 minutes each). If the match is still tied after extra time, it goes to a penalty shootout. The knockout stage consists of the round of 16, quarterfinals, semifinals, and the final. There's also a third-place match between the losers of the semifinals.

- **Number of matches:** If a team makes it all the way to the final, they play a total of seven matches (three in the group stage, one in the round of 16, one in the quarterfinals, one in the semifinals, and one in the final).

This structure allows for a monthlong festival of football, with the 2014 tournament taking place from June 12 to July 13. The 2014 FIFA World Cup was hosted by Brazil, with matches taking place in 12 cities across the country.

The German national team's journey through the 2014 FIFA World Cup tournament was nothing short of a masterclass in precision, teamwork, and the power of sports science.

The tournament began with the group stage, where Germany was drawn into Group G alongside Portugal, Ghana, and the United States. Their opening match against Portugal was a resounding success, with German ace Thomas Müller scoring a hat trick in a 4-0 victory. This was followed by a more challenging match against Ghana that ended in a 2-2 draw, with goals from Mario Götze and Miroslav Klose. The final group match saw Germany secure a 1-0 victory over the United States, with Müller again finding the back of the net.

Advancing to the round of 16, Germany faced Algeria. It was a tense match that went into extra time, but goals from the forward, André Schürrle, and the midfielder, Mesut Özil, secured a 2-1 victory for Germany.

In the quarterfinals, Germany faced France. In a tightly contested match, a header from defender Mats Hummels was enough for Germany to secure a 1-0 victory and a place in the semifinals.

The semifinal against Brazil is one that will live long in the memory of football fans around the world. Germany stunned the host nation with a 7-1 victory, with goals from forwards Thomas Müller and Miroslav Klose and midfielder Sami Khedira, as well as a remarkable four goals from forward André Schürrle and midfielder Toni Kroos combined. This match demonstrated the effectiveness of Germany's team play and their clinical finishing.

The final against Argentina was a tense affair, with both teams having chances to win in regular time. However, it was a substitute, forward Mario Götze, who made the difference in the 113th minute of extra time. He controlled a cross from fellow forward André Schürrle with his chest before volleying the ball into the net, scoring the only goal of the match and securing Germany's fourth World Cup title.

The German Football Association (DFB) has long been recognized for its passion for innovation and forward-thinking approach to sports science. They were one of the first national teams to recognize the potential of scientific methods to enhance player performance and team success. Sports science is deeply integrated with Germany's footballing philosophy, with every part of their operations infused with sports science, from player development and training to injury prevention and recovery. Throughout the tournament, the German team demonstrated the power of teamwork, tactical discipline, and the effective use of sports science in optimizing player performance. Their victory was a testament to their skill, preparation, and strategic use of data in modern football.

For the 2014 FIFA World Cup, the DFB collaborated with SAP, a fellow German corporation and leading software company, to develop a unique football analytics tool known as SAP Match Insights. This tool was designed to enhance the performance of the German national team by providing a detailed analysis of training, preparation, and matches. This tool's insights allowed the German team to analyze vast amounts of data from on-field performance. It tracked player movements and ball possession, providing metrics such as speed, distance covered, and positioning. This data was then made available to coaches and players in an easy-to-understand format, enabling them to gain insights into their performance and make data-driven decisions.

SAP Match Insights captured data in several ways to provide the team with a competitive advantage during the 2014 FIFA World Cup:

- **Player tracking:** The tool used video feeds from matches and training sessions to track player movements. This data was then analyzed to provide insights into various aspects of the team's performance, such as player positioning, ball possession, and player interactions.

- **Performance metrics:** SAP Match Insights was able to measure key performance metrics such as the distance covered by each player, their speed, and their work rate. This information was crucial in assessing player fitness and performance levels, which helped in making decisions about player substitutions and managing player workloads.

- **Data visualization:** The tool presented the data in an easy-to-understand visual format, which made it easier for the coaching staff and players to understand and use the information. This included heat maps showing player movements and areas of the pitch where key actions took place, as well as charts and graphs showing various performance metrics.

- **Collaborative analysis:** SAP Match Insights also provided a platform for players and coaches to collaborate and communicate about the data. They could share videos, comment on specific play sequences, and discuss strategies based on the data.

By capturing and analyzing this data, SAP Match Insights provided the German team with valuable insights that helped them optimize their performance, develop effective game strategies and ultimately win the 2014 FIFA World Cup. The tool was used to facilitate communication and information sharing between players and coaches. It helped the German team to improve their performance by identifying strengths and weaknesses, optimizing training, and developing game strategies.

The key areas that Germany focused on in their application of sports science were as follows:

- **Player fitness:** The DFB strongly emphasizes player fitness. They utilize advanced tracking technologies and data analytics to monitor players' physical condition and tailor individual training programs. This approach ensures that each player is at their physical peak for every match. For example, through a sports science–based tailored training program and a carefully managed diet, Thomas Müller, Germany's star midfielder, was able to maintain high energy levels throughout the tournament. He completed the 2014 FIFA World Cup campaign scoring five goals and providing three key assists. As a team, in the 2014 World Cup, Germany covered an average of 113 kilometers per game, significantly higher than the tournament average of 105 kilometers. The sports science team models for each player were so precise that during the quarterfinal match against France, Miroslav Klose was substituted in the 69th minute after data indicated that he was fatigued. He was replaced by Andre Schürrle, providing the team with fresh energy and helping to secure Germany's victory.

- **Injury prevention:** The DFB uses sports science to minimize the risk of injuries. By analyzing data from training and matches, they can identify potential injury risks and take preventive measures. This includes personalized training routines, physiotherapy sessions, and rest periods. This was highlighted, to the rest of the football world's amazement, in the return of Sami Khedira to the 2014 World Cup squad. Khedira's recovery from a serious injury just months before the World Cup is a prime example of the DFB's approach to injury prevention and recovery. Through a sports science–driven recovery program, Khedira was able to return to full fitness from a torn right knee ACL injury in time for the tournament. He played a crucial role in Germany's victory, also scoring Germany's fifth goal against Brazil in their 7-1 semifinal victory of the tournament. To further illustrate the efficacy of the DFB's injury prevention discipline, during the 2014 World Cup, the German team reported only 5 injuries, compared to the tournament average of 12 injuries per team.

- **Nutrition:** Recognizing the role of nutrition in player performance and recovery, the DFB employs a team of nutritionists to provide players with personalized meal plans. These plans are designed to optimize energy levels, aid recovery, and maintain optimal health. This is highly evident in the team performance that the German squad displayed throughout the FIFA 2014 World Cup tournament. The consistent overall performance of the German team throughout the tournament demonstrates the effectiveness of the DFB's sports science approach. Despite the challenging conditions in Brazil, the team maintained high levels of physical performance, with few injuries and consistent energy levels. The German team's nutrition strategy was credited with helping them maintain high energy levels, even in the later stages of matches. Philipp Lahm, fullback for the German squad, was one of the oldest players in the tournament at 30 years old. He was able to maintain a high level of performance throughout the tournament, thanks to a personalized training and nutrition regime that was based on the data uncovered through the team's use of sports science.

Sports science has gradually become part of the competitive sports landscape since its inception in the early 1900s. People started to understand how diet, physiology, and biomechanics could help improve the level of athletic performance—but it wasn't until technology advanced that sports science saw true progress and wide adoption throughout all levels of football.

In the 1980s and 1990s, sports teams and individuals increasingly began hiring sports scientists, analysts, and physiologists to complement their team of coaches in order to gain a competitive advantage. The use of data analytics, performance monitoring systems, and several strategies for recovery became more commonplace. This period marked a shift from relying on intuition to basing decisions on principles backed by evidence and then to data-driven decision-making.

The impact of sports science on football has been profound. It has revolutionized the way teams train, strategize, play, and recover:

- **Training:** Sports science has transformed how football teams approach training. Training programs are now designed based on scientific principles and are tailored to the individual needs of each player. Factors such as player fitness, injury history, and position-specific requirements are considered, ensuring optimal preparation for matches.

- **Performance analysis:** The use of data analytics in football has provided teams with detailed insights into player and team performance. Metrics such as distance covered, sprint speed, and pass accuracy are tracked and analyzed, providing valuable information that can influence tactical decisions.

- **Injury prevention and recovery:** Sports science has significantly improved the way football teams manage injuries. Through the use of advanced monitoring systems, teams can identify injury risks and implement preventive measures. Moreover, sports science has enhanced the recovery process, with personalized recovery programs and advanced physiotherapy techniques reducing the time players spend on the sidelines.

- **Nutrition and hydration:** The role of diet in player performance and recovery has been brought to the forefront by sports science. Teams now employ nutritionists to ensure players are fueling their bodies correctly, with personalized meal and hydration plans becoming the norm.

Through these changes, sports science has not only enhanced the performance of individual players but also influenced the tactical approaches of teams, the management of player health, and the overall spectacle of the game. The game of football, as we know it today, has been significantly shaped by the advancements in sports science. The methods that the DBF team used to emerge victorious created a model for success that other football associations around the world have sought to emulate. The 2014 FIFA World Cup saw data analysis come to the fore as a crucial aspect of modern football. The insights gained from data analysis allowed teams to make more informed decisions, leading to improved performance and, in the case of the German team, ultimate victory.

The field of sports science is characterized by the use of a wide array of tools and techniques, each designed to enhance some aspect of athletic performance. These tools range from sophisticated tracking systems that monitor physical activity to advanced software that analyzes performance data. Tools such as GPS tracking systems to track players on the pitch, heart rate monitors to gauge fatigue levels scientifically, and sleep tracking devices to ensure optimal recovery for their athletes are some of the groundbreaking tools used during the FIFA 2014 World Cup that are standard across all of football today.

The goal of sports science is to provide a comprehensive understanding of an athlete's performance, enabling tailored training programs, effective injury prevention strategies, and optimized recovery protocols. The 2014 FIFA World Cup was a testament to the power of sports science in shaping the outcome of major sporting events. Germany's victory was not only a triumph of skill, strategy, and teamwork but also a testament to their comprehensive, data-driven approach to training, performance optimization, and injury management. The German use of sports science ensured that all their players were at their physical peak for each match, contributing significantly to the team's overall success. The 2014 FIFA World Cup highlighted to the world of football and beyond the potential sports science has to transform this beautiful game. By leveraging the power of data and technology, teams can optimize performance, prevent injuries, and enhance recovery—ultimately leading to improved outcomes on the pitch and for the fans in the stands.

Looking ahead, it's clear that sports science will continue to play an increasingly important role in football and sports in general. As technology continues to advance, we can expect to see even more sophisticated tools and techniques being used to monitor and enhance athletic performance. For instance, artificial intelligence, could provide even deeper insights into player performance, enabling even more personalized training programs. Virtual and augmented reality technologies could be used to enhance training and tactical preparation, providing players with immersive and realistic training scenarios. As our understanding of human physiology and performance continues to grow, sports science will likely play a crucial role in translating these insights into practical applications. This could lead to new approaches to training, recovery, and injury prevention, further enhancing the performance of athletes.

The 2014 FIFA World Cup was a watershed moment in the world of football, showcasing the transformative power of sports science in shaping the outcomes of one of the world's most-watched sporting events. Behind the scenes, a legion of sports scientists, data analysts, and performance experts worked tirelessly, leveraging cutting-edge technology and scientific principles to give their teams a competitive edge. The tournament served as a compelling testament to the potential of science to enhance athletic performance and influence the trajectory of matches. The German national team, in particular, emerged as a prime example of this trend. Their success was not just a product of the skill and talent of their players but also a testament to their strategic investment in sports science.

Germany's approach was comprehensive and meticulously planned. They recognized the value of data in informing their strategies and decisions and invested in tools and technologies that allowed them to capture and analyze this data. SAP Match Insights, the software developed in collaboration with SAP that provided real-time data on player performance, was instrumental in their World Cup campaign. The software solution provided invaluable insights that informed tactical decisions, player substitutions, and training regimens.

In addition to data analysis, the German team also focused on optimizing player health and performance. They developed individualized nutrition plans for each player, ensuring their dietary intake was tailored to their specific needs and performance goals. They also used high-tech compression suits designed to enhance recovery and reduce the risk of injury. These strategies paid off handsomely, with Germany clinching the World Cup title. Their success underscored the potential of sports science to tip the scales in favor of teams that embrace it.

As we gaze into the future, the role of sports science in football and, indeed, in all sports is poised for unprecedented growth. The lessons learned, and the advancements made in the field are not confined to the boundaries of the football pitch but have far-reaching implications across a multitude of sports disciplines.

The insights gleaned from sports science research are becoming a cornerstone in the strategy of sports clubs and organizations around the globe. These insights, often derived from meticulous data analysis and innovative technological applications are enabling these entities to devise and implement strategies that nurture top-tier talent more effectively and cost-efficiently. The ability to analyze performance data in real time, monitor physiological parameters, and tailor training and recovery protocols to individual athletes are revolutionizing the way talent is developed and managed.

The 2014 FIFA World Cup served as a powerful testament to the potential of sports science. It was a window into a future where sports and science are inextricably intertwined, a future where data-driven decisions and scientifically informed strategies are the norm rather than the exception. The success of the German national team, with their comprehensive and strategic embrace of sports science, provided a compelling blueprint for other teams and sports to follow.

But this is just the beginning. As we move forward, the role of science in sports is set to become even more pivotal. It will continue to drive innovation, pushing the boundaries of what is possible in terms of athlete performance, injury prevention, and recovery. It will enhance our understanding of the physiological and psychological demands of different sports, enabling us to optimize training methodologies and performance strategies.

Moreover, the impact of sports science extends beyond the elite level. The principles and methodologies developed in the professional arena can be applied at all levels of sport, from grassroots to amateur competitions. This democratization of sports science has the potential to enhance participation, performance, and enjoyment of sports for all.

In drawing this chapter to a close, it becomes increasingly evident that the future of sports is one where science is not just an adjunct but a central, integral player. The tightly coupled relationship between sports and science, a relationship that was validated during the 2014 FIFA World Cup, is poised to redefine the landscape of sports in ways we are only beginning to comprehend, even today.

This convergence is set to be the driving force behind a wave of innovation that will permeate every facet of sports. From the development of advanced performance analytics tools to the creation of personalized training regimens based on genetic profiles, science will push the boundaries of what is currently deemed possible in sports.

Performance enhancement, a key objective in all sports, will be significantly influenced by this scientific revolution. Athletes will be able to tap into a wealth of data-driven insights to optimize their training, improve their techniques, and maximize their performance on the field, court, track, or pool. The role of guesswork and intuition will give way to evidence-based decision-making, leading to more predictable and improved outcomes. But the impact of this convergence goes beyond performance enhancement. It promises to transform our understanding of sports at a fundamental level. It will shed light on the complex interplay of physiological, psychological, and environmental factors that influence athletic performance. It will provide answers to questions that have long puzzled sports scientists, coaches, and athletes alike.

Moreover, the coming together of sports and science will change the way we participate in and enjoy sports. It will make sports more accessible and inclusive, breaking down barriers and creating opportunities for people of all ages, abilities, and backgrounds. It will enhance the spectator experience, with fans gaining a deeper understanding of the game and having access to a wealth of information and insights that were previously the preserve of professionals.

In essence, the future of sports is a future where science is at the heart of everything—shaping strategies, informing decisions, enhancing performance, and transforming experiences. The 2014 FIFA World Cup was a glimpse into this future, where the power of sports and the potential of science converge to create a new era in sports. It's a time when the thrill of discovery matches the thrill of competition, and the light of scientific knowledge guides the pursuit of excellence.

CHAPTER 3

Social Media Takes
the Olympics by Storm

2016 Rio Olympics: The Refugee Olympic Team Is the Winner

August 5, 2016, was a picture-perfect day in Rio de Janeiro. However, this was no ordinary August day; this was the day the world had been waiting for, the day that Brazil had been feverishly preparing for and the day that history was about to be made. This was the Opening Ceremony to the 2016 Rio Olympics.

The infectious beat of Brazilian Samba music filled the air from the favelas on the hilltops and surrounding neighborhoods, rising to a thunderous clash of music and cheering crowds in the Maracanã Stadium. This monument to athletic history in the heart of Rio de Janeiro was alive! Hundreds of thousands of adoring fans packed the stadium inside and out for this joyous occasion, and their voices rang out loud and proud into the Rio evening. The Maracanã Stadium, or Estádio do Maracanã, as it is known locally, stood tall and proud as a brilliant light shining under the watchful eye of 30-meter-tall awe-inspiring Christ the Redeemer Statue, high on top of Corcovado mountain. This was the center of the Olympic universe, which the sporting world was set up to revolve around for the next 16 days, taking the world on a sporting and cultural journey across Brazil.

The air inside Maracanã Stadium was thick with excitement, a palpable electrical charge that connected the thousands gathered within the stadium, and millions tuned in on television sets and streaming on smart devices from each corner of the world. The crowd was a heartwarming display of diversity and unity, representing our world. This crowd, singing and dancing in unison, was an assortment of languages, cultures, and colors. Wave after wave of cheers rose loudly from the crowd like the waves washing up on Rio's famed beaches. As the broadcast cameras panned across the audience and captured every possible angle of the exhilarating spectacle, the whole world had a front-row seat to bear witness to history being written.

For Brazil, the opportunity to host the Olympics was an occasion of historic proportions. This wasn't merely a matter of organizing a colossal sports event on their soil—an event that, up until that point, had never before been held anywhere in South America. The significance of this monumental undertaking extended far beyond just providing a stage for athletes hailing from 207 nations to compete across an incredible array of 28 different sports, totaling an unprecedented 306 events. This was a unique chance for Brazil to unfold the rich tapestry of its cultural beauty before the eyes of the world.

The Olympics became a backdrop against which Brazil could showcase the vibrant spirit of its people, a spirit steeped in infectious samba rhythms, a rainbow of traditions, and an irrepressible zest for life. It was an opportunity to broadcast the Brazilian population's unquestionable love for life, a love reflected in their passion for music, their celebration of diversity, and their capacity to find joy in the simplest things. It was a chance to show their unfaltering resilience, a resilience built on a history of overcoming adversities and challenges and a testament to their collective courage.

As the world tuned in to watch, Brazil seized the moment to shed the shadows of economic uncertainty and political turbulence that had dogged it in recent times. The nation stepped proudly into the global limelight, presenting to the world an unforgettable spectacle that was so uniquely Brazilian. Despite the complexities and controversies that brewed in the background, Brazil harnessed the power of unity, channeling the collective strength of its diverse people to stage an event that captured the hearts and imaginations of viewers worldwide.

This was more than just a sporting event; it was a demonstration of Brazil's infectious and famous love for life. Their warmth, hospitality, and effervescent spirit shone through every event and every ceremony, transforming the Games into a festival of human spirit and resilience.

The power of sport merged with the pulse of a nation, creating a mesmerizing spectacle that echoed the vibrant lifeblood of Brazil, speaking of unity, strength, and an enduring passion for life that is emblematic of this South American nation. The Olympics, a gathering of nations, a celebration of human strength and spirit, was about to unfold. The vision was clear—a harmonious fusion of sports and culture, an exhibition of the extraordinary things human beings are capable of when they push the boundaries of their potential. The honor of participating as an Olympian was the culmination of years of relentless hard work, a testament to resilience, and an emblem of global unity in the pursuit of excellence.

As the lights, cameras, and fans beamed down on the Opening Ceremony about to begin at Maracanã Stadium, the stage was set for the world to experience something that they had never before experienced. The 2016 Rio Olympics, officially known as the Games of the XXXI Olympiad was a beacon of hope, a testimony to the transformative power of sports, and as the Opening Ceremony unfolded, it was clear that it would be an Olympics like no other that had come before it.

In an explosion of color and sound, the Opening Ceremony of the 2016 Rio Olympics took us on a journey into Brazil's rich history of art and culture The stage transformed into a breathtaking display of light and shadow, capturing the heart and soul of Brazilian essence. Music, that lifeblood of Brazilian spirit, ebbed and flowed throughout the stadium, carrying with it the energy of dance. The air was filled with the resonating beat of percussion, the infectious strum of flamenco guitars, the sultry allure of the bossa nova and samba. The rhythm of a thousand swaying bodies, both on the stage and in the stands, each lost in the enchantment of dance.

The spectacle unfolded with the perfect timing and choreography of a Broadway theater production, each scene a masterpiece woven into the elaborate ceremony. Cutting-edge light shows danced across the stage, creating magical images of Portuguese explorers carving their way through the lush Amazonian jungles. Here, the indigenous tribes and these foreign sojourners met and melded, creating a haunting tableau of Brazil's early history. In a powerful narrative turn, the host country courageously chose not to shy away from the darker chapters of its history. A somber moment descended as the stadium bore witness to the depiction of millions of enslaved Africans, whose lives were wrenched away and whose sweat and blood seeped into the very soil of Brazil over centuries.

Then, out of the shadow of the past, a new image emerged, the image of a nation driving headfirst into modernity. The stage morphed into a metropolis, with acrobats soaring above to symbolize the skyscrapers of Brazil's mega-cities, their twinkling lights a testament to Brazil's relentless march toward progress. Finally, the ceremony culminated in a sobering call to action against global warming. This grand spectacle of lights, music, art, and dance receded, giving way to a stark tableau underscoring the imminent danger of climate change. The ceremony didn't end with a huge climactic finale but with a question left lingering in the air: would we, the world, leave the catastrophe that looms before us unchecked? The Opening Ceremony, a celebration of life and humanity, concluded with a plea for our collective home. This provided a reminder to the millions who had tuned in, that the future of our planet hinges on our collective actions today.

With the world watching, 10 extraordinary individuals marched out of the legendary Maracanã Stadium after the Opening Ceremony. Representing no country, these 10 athletes represented the struggles and dreams of millions. Stepping into the spotlight, they became symbols of the unwavering human spirit. This was the Refugee Olympic Team—a team that knows no borders or nationalities but is instead a reminder of our common humanity. In those unforgettable moments, the Refugee Olympic Team athletes, originally hailing from four countries engulfed in a humanitarian crisis—Syria, South Sudan, Ethiopia, and the Democratic Republic of Congo—took center stage. These athletes had overcome the unimaginable and journeyed from the farthest reaches of hardship and hopelessness to make it to the world stage. They did not stand proudly under the colors of any single or combined national flag; they carried the flag with the immediately recognizable five-ringed banner of the Olympics. The image was simple, yet the message was powerful and transformative. Their presence loudly shouted that even though they lacked a country to call their own, they did not lack a voice, and they did not lack spirit, resilience, or determination—that is the hallmark of humanity and the Olympic Games.

That moment will be forever etched into the annals of history. The moment that the Refugee Olympic Team took to the stage ahead of the host nation, Brazil, in the Opening Ceremony march, led by Rose Nathike Lokonyen, a 23-year-old South Sudanese runner, the applause was deafening. Their entry into the stadium was seen by millions around the world, immediately raising global awareness of the refugee crisis. United Nations High Commissioner for Refugees, Filippo Grandi, had this to say about that historical moment:

"I was so nervous, waiting for them and I was really, how can I say, full of expectation how the crowd, the huge crowd of the Maracanã Stadium would react, and I must say I wasn't disappointed, because when the Refugee Team was announced by the speaker in three languages, everybody stood up and clapped. And it says a lot about the strength of solidarity, not just in this country, but worldwide."

Each one of those 10 individuals was so much more than just an athlete. They were the embodiment of human resilience, living proof that hope could be kindled amidst the turmoil of a global crisis. Their trials and triumphs were more than personal narratives; they represented the shared experiences of refugees worldwide. They were no longer just individual athletes but an iconic team; they became a beacon of hope, courage, and resilience for millions of people around the world. As they took their strides on the global stage, they also stepped into the hearts of millions worldwide, creating a lasting impression of their bravery in the face of adversity and of their message of hope. As they competed under the five-ringed banner of the Olympics, the world did not just watch a sporting event; it bore witness to a powerful statement of solidarity and a testament to the transformative power of sports. Through their grit and determination, these athletes sparked a dialogue on a global scale, offering a new perspective on the refugee crisis and illuminating the shared humanity that connects us all.

The Refugee Olympic Team's formation was a response to the escalating global refugee crisis. At the start of 2016, Grandi reported that the number of displaced individuals worldwide had surpassed 65 million, the highest it had been since World War II. The International Olympic Committee (IOC) wanted to make a powerful statement about this crisis and the plight of refugees worldwide. The idea behind the creation of a Refugee Olympic Team came from IOC President Thomas Bach, who saw it as an opportunity to raise awareness of the issue and to give refugees around the world a symbol of hope. On March 2, 2016, the IOC Executive Board officially approved the creation of the Refugee Olympic Team. The IOC then started the process of identifying potential athletes among the millions of displaced people around the world. The prerequisites were that the athletes must be refugees, they should have Olympic-level skill in their sport, and they should represent the values of the Olympics.

Thomas Bach, a former West German Olympic fencer and a gold medalist in the team foil event at the 1976 Montreal Olympics, took office as the IOC president in 2013. He was deeply moved by the escalating global refugee crisis and saw the creation of a Refugee Olympic Team as a way for the IOC to send a powerful message of support to displaced people around the world. He believed in the potential of sports to bring about social integration, foster understanding, and advocate for the rights and dignity of marginalized populations.

Upon gaining approval from the IOC Executive Board for the creation of the Refugee Olympic Team, Bach personally led the task of identifying potential athletes among refugees worldwide, arranging for their training, and finalizing the selection of the team members. After months of intensive search, the IOC identified 43 potential athletes. These athletes went through a training and selection process, and finally, in June 2016, the IOC officially announced the final composition of the Refugee Olympic Team for the Rio Olympics. The 10 athletes would compete in three sports: Athletics (track and field), judo, and swimming. The leadership and conviction of Bach played an instrumental role in the formation and success of the Refugee Olympic Team, marking a significant milestone in the history of the Olympics. His initiative reflected the spirit of the Olympic Charter, which states, "The goal of Olympism is to place sport at the service of the harmonious development of humankind, with a view to promoting a peaceful society concerned with the preservation of human dignity."

The inclusion of the Refugee Olympic Team in the 2016 Rio Olympics was a conscious, deliberate act that carried immense symbolic weight. It was a testament to the Olympic ideals of unity and camaraderie and an echo of the ancient Olympic Truce, calling for a cessation of conflict, and a plea for peace. The IOC was not just giving these 10 athletes a chance to compete; they were providing them a platform to bring the plight of refugees to the forefront of global consciousness. The inclusion of the team was a powerful statement that sports can transcend politics and conflict. It was an affirmation that everyone—regardless of their origins, race, or social status—deserves a chance to realize their dreams and potentials.

The Refugee Olympic Team was made up of the athletes listed in Table 3.1.

Table 3.1: The Refugee Olympic Team

ATHLETE	ORIGINALLY FROM	SPORT	EVENT/ CATEGORY
Yusra Mardini	Syria	Swimming	Women's 100m freestyle
			Women's 100m butterfly

ATHLETE	ORIGINALLY FROM	SPORT	EVENT/ CATEGORY
Rami Anis	Syria	Swimming	Men's 100m butterfly
			Men's 100m freestyle
Yiech Pur Biel	South Sudan	Athletics	Men's 800m
James Nyang Chiengjiek	South Sudan	Athletics	Men's 400m
Yonas Kinde	Ethiopia	Athletics	Men's marathon
Anjelina Nadai Lohalith	South Sudan	Athletics	Women's 1500m
Rose Nathike Lokonyen	South Sudan	Athletics	Women's 800m
Paulo Amotun Lokoro	South Sudan	Athletics	Men's 1500m
Yolande Bukasa Mabika	Democratic Republic of Congo	Judo	Women's 70kg
Popole Misenga	Democratic Republic of Congo	Judo	Men's 90kg

Each athlete on the Refugee Olympic Team carried with them a compelling story of struggle, survival, and pure grit. Each of their countries had been, and continued to be, ravaged by conflicts and humanitarian crises. These incredible individuals endured the trauma of being forced to flee their homelands, the only homes they knew, and faced an uncertain future in refugee camps. Yusra Mardini and Rami Anis, both swimmers, fled the war-torn landscapes of Syria. Mardini's story of pulling a sinking boat to safety on her journey to Europe became emblematic of the team's indomitable spirit. Six athletes—Yiech Pur Biel, James Nyang Chiengjiek, Anjelina Nadai Lohalith, Rose Nathike Lokonyen, Paulo Amotun Lokoro, and Yonas Kinde—left behind conflict in South Sudan and Ethiopia. Judo competitors Yolande Bukasa Mabika and Popole Misenga found asylum from the Democratic Republic of Congo's struggles.

Yet amidst all the chaos, these athletes held onto their dreams of sporting glory. For many of them, their exceptional talent was spotted in refugee camps or during their asylum period. With support from the IOC and various other organizations, they were provided the opportunity to train and prepare for the Olympic stage.

While the Refugee Olympic Team did not secure any medals at the Rio Olympics, their participation was a triumph in itself. Each athlete put forth a commendable performance, considering the difficult circumstances under which they trained and prepared. Their participation symbolized a beacon of hope and resilience, telling a story far beyond the competition itself. Their true achievement was not quantifiable by medals or podium finishes. Instead, it was the inspiring journey they undertook, the global awareness they raised about the refugee crisis, and the hearts they touched with their resilient spirit and incredible bravery. Their presence at the 2016 Rio Olympics brought to light the true essence of the Olympic spirit: unity, equality, and the human capacity to overcome adversity.

The athletes' proud march under the bright lights and huge roar from the crowd during the Opening Ceremony was amplified across the globe by another, ever-present light: the gentle flickering of screens. The grand opening of the 2016 Olympics in Rio was amplified around the world by the constant presence of screens, from giant billboards in Times Square to tiny cellphones in far-flung villages thanks to the rise of social media. This was the first Olympics with the full strength of social media behind it; humanity had become aware of how connectedness and collaboration could give power to a single voice. The tools used for this were platforms like Facebook, Twitter, and Instagram. In this new digital version of the Olympics, these digital platforms became global stages, amplifying the events taking place in Rio de Janeiro to a worldwide audience. These platforms offered access to real-time updates, behind-the-scenes glimpses, and exclusive content, bridging the gap between athletes and spectators and making the Games a truly shared international experience. The massive global scale of the 2016 Rio Olympics made it easier for fans to feel closer to the games than ever before; this connectedness drove a truly interactive Olympic experience. Major Olympic sponsors and partners, such as Visa, also supported the Refugee Olympic Team. For example, Visa included the team in their global advertising campaign, "The Caravan," highlighting the athletes' journeys (Visa has a history of philanthropy related to refugee support).

Following along with social media coverage was like following an Olympic reality show, complete with ongoing plot lines and surprise twists that had audiences begging for more. Social media allowed the fans of the Olympics to feel closer to the games than ever before by building support and admiration for countries' individual athletes driving a truly interactive and globally connected experience. In this digital version of the Olympics, the Refugee Olympic Team found an arena that echoed with support and admiration for their cause; news feeds filled with stories about their triumphs both on and off the field. This was responsible for driving incredible awareness for not only the athletes but of the plight of refugees around the world. Social media helped bring to life the idea born years earlier by Bach, using the power of sport to be a vehicle for driving social change through the massive reach of the Olympic Games.

One of the most significant campaigns that propelled the Refugee Olympic Team into the social media spotlight was the #TeamRefugees initiative. Led by the United Nations and supported by influencers from various fields, the campaign generated widespread attention and support for the team.

Notable personalities, including famous athletes, celebrities, and public figures joined in, sharing messages of solidarity and highlighting the team's extraordinary journey. U.S. President Barack Obama sent this message of support shortly before the Refugee Olympic Team was introduced during the Opening Ceremony:

"Tonight, the first-ever #TeamRefugees will also stand before the world and prove that you can succeed no matter where you're from." Pope Francis sent a letter to the Refugee Team, extending his support: "I extend my greetings and wish you success at the Olympic Games in Rio—that your courage and strength find expression through the Olympic Games and serve as a cry for peace and solidarity."

The global reach of these influencers helped bring the stories of the athletes to a broader audience, reinforcing the narrative of resilience and hope that the team represented. Through social media, the team's journey and the individual stories behind each athlete were readily accessible by billions of connected people around the world. Social media served as a megaphone for so many voices; it helped drive awareness through massive amounts of deeply personal content and gave a global voice to those who previously had no platform to speak through. The hashtags #TeamRefugees and #RefugeeOlympics became viral rallying cries for supporters across the world, generating millions of engagements and shares. The power of these viral hashtags lay not just in their reach but in their ability to unite individuals globally around a shared cause.

It was not only the millions of Olympic fans and supporters of the Refugee Team and their mission who took to social media. The athletes themselves used their social influence on these platforms to share personal insights into their experiences, fostering a sense of connection and empathy among their followers. These narratives resonated deeply with audiences worldwide, prompting discussions about the refugee crisis and the role of sport in promoting social change.

The global response to the Refugee Olympic Team via social media was overwhelmingly positive. Audiences worldwide celebrated their stories, expressing admiration for their courage and resilience. Every race they ran or swam and every judo match they fought was met with supportive messages from around the world. It didn't matter where they placed in an event; they were there and so were their supporters—in the multiple Olympic venues across Brazil and online via social media. The Refugee Team became the world's team, no matter which country you supported.

These social media interactions served as more than just tokens of admiration; they represented a profound, global recognition of the realities refugees grapple with. As each like, share, or retweet reverberated across the Internet, the narrative of the refugee crisis was being told in corners of the globe that had previously been untouched by their tales. Every tweet, like, or share became a testament to the unifying power of sports, an affirmation of the belief that sports have the ability to break barriers, inspire change, and unite people. These platforms morphed into digital arenas where the world could witness the athletes' trials and triumphs, creating a ripple effect that reverberated across the globe, inspiring and rallying for change.

The global conversations sparked by the team's presence at the Games shed light on the power of sport as a tool for promoting social integration and advocating for the rights of marginalized populations. By giving voice to these athletes, social media became a powerful platform for change, underscoring the belief that sport has the power to unite and inspire. The platform amplified the athletes' voices, turning their personal stories into powerful narratives that touched millions. In an increasingly connected world, these digital interactions held the power to transcend cultural and geographical divides, fostering understanding, empathy, and unity. Through the lens of social media, the world saw that these were not just 10 athletes competing in a sports event; they were ambassadors of hope in a world rife with conflict and displacement.

The narrative of the Refugee Olympic Team underscored the belief that sports have the power not only to unite but also to inspire. They have the capacity to transcend the playing field and permeate our collective consciousness, prompting us to reflect, to empathize, and, ultimately, to act. This is the transformative power of sports, a power that, when amplified by the reach of social media, can ignite conversations, drive global awareness, and effect real, meaningful change.

The members of the Refugee Olympic Team in 2016 brought to light a narrative that extended far beyond the confines of the Maracanã Stadium. This team, composed of refugees from around the world, challenged and reshaped the international perception of those who had been displaced from their homes. In an era where so much press has focused on the loss, tragedy, and despair associated with displacement, these athletes showed immense courage and strength in order for the world to glimpse a different story—one of resilience, hope, and possibility. Through their involvement in this iconic sporting event, in addition to their incredible personal stories, they successfully shattered the stereotypes too often associated with refugees. By showcasing their abilities on the global sporting stage, the athletes proved that being a refugee is not a characteristic but rather a circumstance. They reminded the world that refugees are individuals with skills, dreams, and aspirations, capable of remarkable feats given the opportunity. Their story, broadcast and amplified across the world through television, streaming, and virally across social media, brought humanity and understanding to a crisis often reduced to numbers and statistics, urging the world to look beyond the label of "refugee."

The Olympic journey, with its remarkable mix of cultural encounters, personal achievements, and global spotlight, served as a profound catalyst that dramatically altered the course of the 10 athletes' lives. Born and raised in parts of the world that often exist on the periphery of the global consciousness—places relatively unknown, misunderstood, or overlooked—these athletes, who started as unknown refugees, suddenly found themselves standing on a very public international platform. From quiet lives of struggle and resilience, they were catapulted into the very heart of the global stage where every leap, sprint, and dive was closely watched and cheered on by millions around the world. The eyes of an entire planet—its media, its leaders, its citizens—were now firmly focused on and cheering for these 10 unique and inspiring individuals.

The newfound attention they received did not just serve to highlight their athleticism but also cast them into significant roles that went beyond the sporting field. They became de facto international ambassadors, whose influence extended far beyond their personal achievements and identities. They were no longer representing just themselves or their athletic skills. The athletes on the Refugee Olympic Team were now shouldering the responsibility of giving a voice to the collective experiences and struggles of millions of displaced individuals scattered worldwide. From here, they could share their narratives, recount their own experiences and challenges, champion the rights of refugees, and direct global attention toward the urgent, ever-escalating crisis of displacement.

Their stories, their performances, and their lives served as a reminder to the world of the human faces behind the statistics of displacement. Their Olympic journey was not merely about medals and national anthems; it was a poignant call to the world to acknowledge, address, and act upon the refugee crisis that continues to surge across borders and continents. When the excitement of the Olympics eventually died down, many of these athletes chose to maintain their trajectory within the world of sports. Harnessing the power of their newfound fame, they found themselves with access to improved resources and heightened levels of support to further hone their athletic skills. For example, instead of settling into the anonymity that post-Olympics life could offer, Yusra Mardini leveraged her platform to form a partnership with the United Nations High Commissioner for Refugees (UNHCR). The UNHCR is a United Nations program established in 1950 with a mandate to protect and support refugees at the request of a government or the UN itself and assist in their voluntary repatriation, local integration, or resettlement to a third country. Its primary purpose is to safeguard the rights and well-being of refugees and stateless people. In more than six decades, the agency has helped tens of millions of people restart their lives. The UNHCR also has a mandate to help stateless people, a category of individuals who do not have a nationality or legal status. It was in partnership with the UNHCR that Mardini emerged as a potent advocate for refugees around the globe, using her voice to drive change and influence the discourse around refugee rights.

Beyond their sports careers, the athletes' extraordinary journey to and beyond the Olympics also opened a multitude of doors in other spheres of life. Their inspiring, human stories of resilience and triumph against the odds were compelling narratives that touched the hearts and minds of millions across the world. This led to a steady stream of opportunities, including invitations to speaking engagements where they could motivate and inspire others with their lived experiences, book deals, and the chance to collaborate with international organizations committed to providing aid to refugees. Through these diverse avenues, the athletes continue to expand their influence. The athletes continue to make progress, not only in the sports field, where they first gained recognition but in a much larger arena. They have become instrumental in shaping public discourse and attitudes toward refugees, thereby fostering more inclusive societies. It is through these ongoing efforts that the athletes continue to have an impact that reverberates far beyond the confines of a sports stadium, touching the lives of people globally and creating tangible change in our society.

Following the Rio Games, the IOC announced the continuation of the Refugee Olympic Team for future Olympics, providing a platform for talented refugee athletes to compete and represent millions of displaced individuals worldwide. The IOC itself launched the Olympic Refuge Foundation in 2017, in partnership with the United Nations. This organization aims to create safe sports facilities and programs in areas with high concentrations of refugees, ensuring that the legacy of the Refugee Olympic Team translates into tangible support for displaced individuals worldwide.

The IOC continues to field a Refugee Olympic Team in every Olympic Games for a number of compelling reasons:

- **Global awareness:** The Refugee Olympic Team is a powerful tool for raising global awareness about the plight of refugees. By providing these athletes with a platform, the IOC brings attention to the global refugee crisis, fostering understanding and empathy among viewers worldwide.

- **Advocacy and solidarity:** The team serves as a symbol of international solidarity and advocacy for refugee rights. It exemplifies the IOC's commitment to promoting peace and human dignity in alignment with the core principles of Olympism.

- **Empowerment:** The Refugee Olympic Team offers refugee athletes the chance to pursue their athletic dreams and demonstrate their potential despite the adversities they've faced. This opportunity for empowerment can have a transformative impact on their lives.

- **Inclusion and diversity:** The inclusion of the Refugee Olympic Team promotes diversity within the Olympic movement. It signals that the Olympics are a truly global event, open to all, regardless of nationality or personal circumstances.

- **Inspiration:** The resilience and determination of the refugee athletes inspire millions around the world. Their stories of overcoming hardship to compete on the world's biggest sporting stage offer hope and motivation to other displaced individuals.

- **Legacy and continuity:** The continued presence of the Refugee Olympic Team at the Olympics allows for the creation of a lasting legacy, one that acknowledges the ongoing nature of the refugee crisis and encourages a continuity of focus, support, and solutions for this pressing global issue.

By continuing to field a Refugee Olympic Team, the IOC leverages the power of sports to shed light on important social issues, reaffirming the Olympic ideals of unity and peace and the promotion of a better, more inclusive world. This groundbreaking initiative has since inspired other major sporting events to consider similar strategies, recognizing the power of sports as a force for social change and integration. The IOC's bold and progressive move rippled out into the wider world of sports, setting the wheels in motion for other major sporting events to contemplate the integration of similar strategies into their own structures. This signaled a newfound recognition of the transformative power of sports, not just as a display of physical prowess and competitive spirit but as a potent force for social change, integration, and unity.

The legacy of the 2016 Rio Refugee Olympic Team continues to inspire and resonate with millions across the world. It serves as a powerful testament to the ability of sports to transcend geopolitical borders, cultural differences, and socioeconomic barriers. Sports have the potential to empower marginalized populations, including refugees. They foster mutual understanding, nurture global solidarity, and champion the determination and grit of the human spirit. Social media's power to amplify the Refugee Olympic Team's stories turned them into symbols of hope and resilience, fueling a global movement of support for refugees. This newfound recognition endured post-Olympics, with many of these athletes leveraging their social media presence to continue advocating for refugee rights, providing insights into the struggles they face, and inspiring millions worldwide.

Since the 2016 Rio Olympics, the influence of social media has continued to grow seemingly across every single aspect of our lives. Platforms have developed new features that enhance storytelling, drive engagement and consumption, and foster community engagement. Live streaming, for example, allows real-time broadcasting of events with content that is not available anywhere else. Tools for fundraising directly on social media platforms enable effective mobilization of resources for causes. As such, the potential for social media to create a global platform for good has increased exponentially, as has its potential to spotlight crucial issues like the global refugee crisis. This evolution underscores the enduring legacy of the Refugee Olympic Team's impact at the Rio Games and the continuing potential for amplifying their stories in future Olympics.

As we look forward, the lessons from the 2016 Rio Olympics and the Refugee Olympic Team stand as beacons, guiding us toward a world where sport, technology, and a commitment to social change can intertwine to create a more inclusive and understanding global community.

The initiation and continuation of the Refugee Olympic Team by the IOC was not merely a symbolic gesture but a potent stride toward advancing the dialogue on global social issues. The move beautifully blended the realms of sports, advocacy, and storytelling, underpinning the profound potential of sports as a catalyst for social change, peace, and unity. These athletes, displaced from their homelands, found in the Olympics not just a platform to display their athletic prowess, but a unique stage from which they could voice the experiences and challenges of refugees worldwide.

The power of this initiative was further bolstered by the ever-expanding reach and influence of technology (more specifically, social media). As a tool for global communication and mobilization, social media platforms amplified the narratives of the Refugee Olympic Team, transforming them into resonant symbols of hope and resilience. This propelled a global support movement for refugees, which continues to thrive long after the closing ceremony of the 2016 Rio Olympics. With new technological advancements and the continuing evolution of social media, the potential for creating a global platform for good has magnified. The legacy left by the Refugee Olympic Team, both on the field and in the broader sphere of social discourse, illustrates the power of the Olympic movement to inspire change, promote inclusivity, and champion humanitarian causes. This legacy continues to reverberate, promising a bright future where sports are recognized not just as games but as a transformative force that holds the power to shape societies and bring the world closer together.

The Role of Biometric Tech in Shaping the Game

2016 NBA Finals: Cleveland Cavaliers vs. Golden State Warriors

In Deep East Oakland, California, the world-famous Oracle Arena was a pulsing epicenter of anticipation, alive with energy, teeming with a kind of electricity only a Game 7 in the NBA Finals could generate. In every corner of this sports cathedral, the excitement had taken over, an intoxicating blend of anxiety, team spirit, and hope that filled the air. This energy was more than just a simple feeling; it was a palpable entity, an electric charge that swept through the arena like a relentless wave. You could feel it tingling at your fingertips. The buzz of anticipation, the rumble of suspense, the heartbeat of hope—all these swirled together in a captivating symphony that truly embodied the unparalleled magic of Game 7 of the NBA Finals.

There was not a single empty seat to be found in this magnificent colosseum, a testament to the sheer loyalty of the fan base, their devotion unbreakable. They filled every corner, from the nosebleed sections to the million-dollar courtside seats. Fans, dressed in their team colors, painted a moving tableau that mirrored a human kaleidoscope, a living, breathing testament to their unwavering loyalty. It was as if the arena itself had come alive, swaying and pulsating to the rhythm of the crowd's collective heartbeat. The arena was now awash with a sea of diverse colors, a giant mosaic of hopes and dreams stitched together by the shared passion of tens of thousands. It was a captivating scene, one that spoke to the power of sports to bring people together and cheer for a collective goal. It was beautiful. It was breathtaking. It was basketball at its finest.

The decibel level within the arena had reached its crescendo, an almost deafening symphony of pure, undiluted emotion. Each cheer, each chant, and each gasp of anticipation served as a testament to the significance of what was at stake. The resounding echo of fanatical fervor reverberated off the walls, the ceiling, and the floor, transforming the Oracle Arena into a concert of sound and passion.

The stage was set. It was Game 7 of the 2016 NBA Finals. This was not just another game; it was the culmination of blood, sweat, and tears, of dreams nurtured and ambitions pursued. It was the final showdown, the epic clash of titans that would either etch a team into the annals of history or thrust them into the shadows of defeat. There was no middle ground, no second chance, just the sound of the whistle and the relentless tick of the game clock.

This was the moment. This was the pinnacle of excitement, where legends were forged and dynasties were born. This was it!

The Golden State Warriors, a team of immense talent, a well-oiled machine of precision and finesse, stood tall on their home court, a court where they'd danced and dazzled throughout the season, a court where they'd rewritten the very history of the game with an astounding 73-win season. An army led by the superhero, Stephen Curry, they were warriors in every sense, their eyes shining with the spark of champions. Determined to drive one last time to victory.

On the flip side of the court, the Cleveland Cavaliers stood, a team defined by relentless grit and sheer determination. They weren't just playing for themselves; they were carrying the weight of a city, a city that had been thirsting for a championship for more than 50 long, hard years. This was about more than just the game; it was about breaking a decades-old dry spell, about quenching a deep-seated hunger for victory. At the helm was LeBron James, a powerhouse of talent, his leadership as unshakable as his reputation. He was more than just a star player; he was the team's backbone, his fierce resolve echoing through each and every Cavalier, spurring them on to greater heights. The star power that LeBron brought to the game was undeniable, and he was determined to end the Cavaliers' half-century dry spell. Kyrie Irving, LeBron's dynamic counterpart, brought his own brand of fire to the team. Quick and fearless, his unpredictable plays and sharp shooting prowess kept opponents on their toes, his audacity on the court adding a spark to the Cavaliers' lineup.

Despite finding themselves in the deep hole of a 3-1 deficit, the Cavaliers had managed to stage an incredible comeback. It was a story of determination, a testament to the Cavaliers' dogged persistence and unwillingness to bow down to adversity. The spectacle was almost straight out of Hollywood, the kind of gritty, against-all-odds narrative you'd expect from a sports movie, not something you expected to find in real life, let alone the NBA Finals.

Every shot, every rebound, every triumphant cry, the Cavaliers were doing more than just playing basketball. They were defying expectations, rewriting what seemed like an inevitable ending, and pushing against the tides of fate. Their journey was a vivid example of the true power of resilience, a testament to the unwavering spirit of the underdog. As the floodlights bathed the court, shadows and light danced across the faces of these titans. The crowd held its collective breath; the silence punctuated only by the squeak of shoes and the echo of the bouncing ball. This was not just a game; it was a battle of wills, a clash of titans, a moment in history where time stood still. On this day, heroes would be made, legacies would be cemented, and one city would erupt in jubilation. This was the 2016 NBA Finals, and nothing would ever be the same in basketball again.

Basketball, a sport that combines the perfect blend of skill, strategy, and physical prowess, has always been a breeding ground for innovation. One of the latest leaps in technological advancement was the introduction of wearable biometric sensors. These devices, capable of tracking a multitude of physiological parameters, have proven to be game-changers, revolutionizing the way teams approach training, recovery, and in-game strategies.

In 2016, the use of wearable biometric sensors in sports and athletic training began to gain significant traction. These small yet highly sophisticated devices, resembling the simplicity of a wristwatch or a fabric patch, represented a groundbreaking fusion of technology and health science. They played an integral role in the athletic realm, pioneering a fresh approach to how athletes monitored their physical well-being. These pioneering devices were tasked with the crucial job of gathering complex biometric data, such as heart rate, skin temperature, sleep patterns, and overall exertion levels. They meticulously logged and analyzed this information, serving as a 24/7 personal monitor for an athlete's physical state. Each heartbeat, each degree of temperature change, and each variation in sleep patterns was captured, providing a comprehensive snapshot of the athlete's physical condition.

The core objective of these devices was to transform the wealth of data they gathered into a holistic, real-time understanding of an athlete's physical state. It was like having a personal sports scientist, doctor, and data analyst all rolled into one, tirelessly working to ensure the optimal health and performance of the athlete. These innovative devices proved to be invaluable tools for tracking health and enhancing performance. They facilitated the early detection of potential health issues, capturing subtle changes that could be the early warnings of a bigger problem. Their precise measurements could flag potential health risks long before they became serious, helping to avoid unexpected downtime. These wearable biometric sensors were instrumental in performance optimization. They were able to track how the body responded to different levels of exertion, helping athletes understand their personal thresholds and identify their peak performance zones. This insightful data served as a key resource for tailoring effective training regimens and boosting athletic performance.

Moreover, the wearable biometric sensors of 2016 played a vital role in reducing injury risks. By identifying patterns of overuse, fatigue, or stress, they could help predict and prevent potential injuries. This was an essential aspect for athletes, as injuries often resulted in detrimental downtime and could lead to long-term complications. In the rapidly advancing world of sports science, wearable biometric sensors marked a significant step forward for sports scientists, offering athletes a powerful blend of data and practicality. They began the transformation of how athletes trained, paving the way for the even more sophisticated devices of the future.

As the 2016 NBA Finals unfolded, a spectacle of exceptional athleticism and relentless rivalry, the curtain was drawn back to reveal a game-changing phenomenon at play: the strategic deployment of wearable biometric sensors. Set against the thrilling backdrop of a championship clash between the formidable Golden State Warriors and the Cleveland Cavaliers, this technology emerged as a crucial game piece on the chessboard of professional basketball. In this high-stakes contest, each team sought to leverage every potential advantage, a pursuit that brought wearable tech out of the shadows and into the spotlight.

Here, amidst the roar of the crowds and the pulsating rhythm of the game, both teams—the Warriors, characterized by their sharpshooting finesse, and the Cavaliers, renowned for their gritty resilience—embraced these cutting-edge tools as crucial assets in their respective arsenals. These innovative devices, no larger than a wristband, were potent and capable of delivering critical insights that could tip the balance of the game. Monitoring variables such as heart rate, sleep patterns, and recovery times, these wearables provided a unique vantage point into player health and performance. In this fiercely competitive environment, these tools became more than just passive observers; they were active contributors in the quest for championship glory. Armed with data from these devices, coaching staff could devise strategies tailored to their players' unique physiological profiles, maximizing performance and minimizing injury risk.

In this way, the 2016 NBA Finals not only showcased a breathtaking contest of skill and strategy but also became a stage for the groundbreaking integration of technology and sport. The power of wearable biometric sensors for gathering critical athlete data from practice was brought to the forefront, underscoring their potential as essential tools in the dynamic, ever-evolving realm of professional sports.

The Golden State Warriors, a team known not only for their spectacular play but also for their progressive approach to training and health management, adopted devices from renowned companies like Catapult Sports and WHOOP. The Warriors, always on the cutting edge of technology, recognized the invaluable role these devices could play in their pursuit of championship glory.

Catapult Sports, a global leader in sports technology, offered devices that could monitor and evaluate a variety of physical performance metrics. From tracking players' exertion levels during grueling training sessions to monitoring recovery during periods of rest, these gadgets provided an unparalleled depth of insight into the physical status of each player.

Catapult's wearable technology, in the form of a small, lightweight device worn in a vest under the player's jersey, incorporated an array of sophisticated inertial sensors, including accelerometers, gyroscopes, and magnetometers. This technology allowed the Warriors' coaching staff to track an impressive range of player metrics in real time.

The following key metrics were captured by Catapult devices:

- **Player load:** This metric, a proprietary measure by Catapult, indicated the overall physical demand placed on an athlete during a training session or game. By aggregating multidirectional movements into a single figure, player load gave the Warriors' coaching staff a clear indication of workload, informing decisions on training intensity, player rotations, and rest periods.

- **Mechanical stress and impact forces:** Catapult devices could monitor the biomechanical stress exerted on players' bodies, including impact forces. This data was invaluable for athletes' injury prevention, allowing the coaching staff to intervene when abnormal stress levels were detected.

- **Sprinting and movement metrics:** Catapult's wearables tracked metrics such as distance covered, speed, acceleration, deceleration, jumps, and changes in direction. These insights helped the team assess player conditioning, understand their physical strengths and limitations, and tailor training regimens accordingly.

By integrating Catapult's technology into their game strategy, the Warriors were not just gaining an understanding of their players' exertion levels; they were stepping into the future of injury prevention and athlete longevity. The data provided by Catapult informed not only immediate tactical decisions but also long-term strategic plans, ensuring that players could perform at their peak while minimizing their risk of injury.

In tandem with Catapult Sports, the Warriors also integrated WHOOP into their technological lineup. WHOOP, a trailblazer in the realm of performance optimization, specialized in tracking recovery and sleep patterns. WHOOP, unlike other fitness trackers, emphasized recovery as much as exertion. It adopted a holistic view of athletic performance, recognizing that optimal performance is a delicate balance of stress and recovery. The WHOOP strap, worn on the wrist, measured heart rate, heart rate variability, ambient temperature, and movement 100 times per second, every second, all day long.

The following key metrics were captured by WHOOP:

- **Strain:** WHOOP measured strain based on the cardiovascular load endured by the body throughout the day, derived from heart rate data. This metric helped the coaching staff understand how physically demanding a player's day, workout, or game was, guiding decisions on training intensity and game time.

- **Recovery:** By assessing resting heart rate, heart rate variability, and sleep performance, WHOOP generated a recovery score for each athlete. This score was pivotal for understanding how ready a player's body was to perform at its peak. It also informed decisions on player rotations, ensuring that the Warriors always had their best players on the court when it mattered most.

- **Sleep:** WHOOP monitored sleep stages (REM, light, deep), disturbances, and duration to provide a sleep performance score.

Adequate sleep is crucial for physical and cognitive functions, so understanding a player's sleep patterns allows for the implementation of tailored sleep strategies to improve recovery and subsequent performance.

WHOOP provided the Warriors' coaching staff with a wealth of data, painting a comprehensive picture of each player's physiological status. This information was instrumental in managing player workload during training, deciding playing time during games, and devising personalized recovery strategies.

In the high-stakes context of the NBA Finals, where even the smallest advantage could turn the tide, these wearable biometric sensors became an indispensable part of the Warriors' strategy. They provided an extra layer of information, a deeper understanding of the players' physical capabilities and needs. As such, they enabled more effective and personalized training regimens, optimized recovery periods, and provided early warnings of potential injury risks. This marked an exciting era in sports, where data and performance worked in harmony to push the boundaries of what was possible on the court. These wearables captured in-depth data on player load, exertion, and recovery. They provided nuanced insights into each player's physiological status, influencing coaching decisions regarding player substitutions, training adjustments, and strategizing for each game.

Contrasting the Warriors, the Cleveland Cavaliers pinned their technological reliance on the world-renowned Polar heart rate monitors. These wearable sensors, known for their precision and reliability, are specialized in tracking the nuanced dance of heart rate variability. This was a vital biometric indicator, a key to unlocking a deeper understanding of each player's physical condition. *Heart rate variability*, or the variation in time between consecutive heartbeats, offered crucial insights into an athlete's state of fatigue and stress. A decrease in heart rate variability could indicate increased stress or insufficient recovery, signals that would otherwise go unnoticed without the aid of this advanced technology.

The value proposition of Polar devices centered around providing robust, real-time physiological data, enabling the coaching staff to fine-tune player training, recovery, and game strategy.

Unlike traditional fitness trackers that measure a single data point, Polar's heart rate monitors captured continuous heart rate data, delivering a nuanced, dynamic view of an athlete's performance and physiological state. By collecting this data during both games and training sessions, the Cavaliers were able to measure and monitor each player's individual and total workloads with precision.

The following key metrics were captured by Polar heart rate monitors:

- **Heart rate variability:** Heart rate variability, the variation in time between each heartbeat, is a reliable indicator of physiological stress and recovery status. Higher heart rate variability often indicates better health and fitness levels. By tracking heart rate variability, the Cavaliers' coaching staff could gauge how well each player was recovering from previous exertions, allowing them to individualize training loads and optimize recovery protocols.

- **Training load:** By monitoring heart rate data throughout each training session and game, Polar devices provided insights into the intensity and volume of physical exertion. This allowed the coaching staff to better understand the impact of different activities on each player's body and adjust training schedules accordingly, aiming to reach peak performance for game time.

- **Recovery status:** By combining training load data with long-term monitoring of resting and overnight heart rate and heart rate variability, Polar's devices could provide an estimate of an athlete's overall recovery status. This insight guided decisions around player rotations, rest periods, and load management, ensuring players were at their physical best when it mattered most.

Armed with this critical data, the Cavaliers' coaching staff was equipped to gauge player fatigue in real time. This allowed them to understand when a player might be pushing beyond their optimal performance threshold, risking not just immediate game performance but also potential long-term health repercussions. In the fast-paced environment of an NBA Finals game, managing player rotations is a strategic chess match. Knowledge of player fatigue and stress levels added an extra layer to this game, enabling more informed decisions about when to rest a player or when to push them for a key play. This ensured that the best possible team was always on the court, balancing individual player strength with overall team performance. The ability to monitor stress levels also impacted the intensity of the game. Understanding each player's stress responses enabled the coaching staff to control the intensity of their plays, ensuring they maximized performance without pushing players into the red zone of exhaustion or injury risk.

Recovery periods, both within and between games, were another crucial element that could be strategically managed based on insights from the Polar heart rate monitors. Optimal recovery is as critical to performance as the training itself, and being able to quantify recovery helped ensure each player was getting the right amount of rest to restore their peak performance capabilities. The Cleveland Cavaliers, much like their counterparts, leveraged the power of wearable biometric technology in their quest for championship glory. By utilizing Polar heart rate monitors, they gained a deeper understanding of their players' fatigue and stress levels, allowing them to make more informed strategic decisions and optimize player performance. This marked yet another example of the revolutionary integration of sports and technology, demonstrating how a smart blend of data and human performance could take athletic performance to new heights.

The team MVP of the 2016 NBA Finals were the wearable biometric sensors that played an unseen yet pivotal role. They bridged the gap between physical intuition and empirical evidence, enabling teams to tailor their strategies based on individual player data. These groundbreaking technologies exemplified the synergy of sports and science, adding a new dimension to the already multifaceted game of basketball. However, in 2016, the NBA did not allow the use of such devices during official games, because of a rule present in the collective bargaining agreement between the NBA and the NBA Players Association. However, teams could use these devices in training sessions and practices. Furthermore, any data gathered through these devices was strictly regulated. The league stipulated that it could be used only for improving players' health and performance, not for negotiations during contract discussions.

Wearable biometric sensors served as the bridge between the raw physicality of the game and the precise, data-driven realm of empirical evidence. They provided a window into the unseen, converting the intangible nuances of player fatigue, stress, and performance into tangible, actionable data. This unprecedented access to real-time biometric data allowed teams to move beyond relying solely on subjective observations and gut feelings, empowering them with objective, evidence-based insights. As a result, teams were able to tailor their strategies to a degree previously unimaginable. Player rotations, game intensity, recovery periods—each aspect could be adjusted based on the individual biometric data from each player. This was an era of personalized strategy, where decisions were data-informed, precise, and finely tuned to each player's unique physiological profile.

In the 2016 NBA Finals, the silent yet powerful role of wearable biometric sensors stood as a shining testament to the incredible synergy of sports and science. They represented the burgeoning trend of technology-infused sports, where science was no longer confined to the laboratory but was integrated into the very fabric of the game. Basketball, a game already rich in strategic depth and physical dynamism, found a new dimension with the adoption of these groundbreaking technologies. The court became a live laboratory, where every move was data, and every player a unique study in performance and resilience. The 2016 NBA Finals thus marked a transformative moment in the world of sports, highlighting the growing significance of wearable biometric sensors in shaping the future of athletic performance.

While the benefits of wearable fitness trackers and biometric sensors were abundantly clear in the high-stakes arena of professional basketball, their use was not without its challenges and concerns. Like many sports organizations worldwide, the NBA found itself embarking on a complex balancing act. It was the juncture of technology's forward march and the need to preserve the sanctity of privacy, data ownership, and competitive fairness. The year 2016 saw the NBA navigating these uncharted waters, grappling with the implications of a world where an athlete's every heartbeat could be quantified and scrutinized. This necessitated the establishment of specific regulations concerning the use of wearable technology within the game's boundaries, a pivotal development that embodied the intersection of sports, law, and emerging tech. Under the stipulations of the collective bargaining agreement, the use of wearable devices during official games was deemed off-limits. This rule was carefully enshrined within the collective bargaining agreement, reflecting the need to ensure competitive fairness and to keep the game grounded in human skill and strategy, untouched by real-time technological aid. Yet, the NBA recognized the immense value these devices offered. Consequently, their use was permitted during training sessions and practices, serving as silent observers and consultants, their data assisting in honing player health and optimizing performance.

As the world of sports continued its tryst with wearable technology, these regulations erected by the NBA served as a crucial guiding beacon. They offered a blueprint for negotiating the intricate maze where sports, technology, and privacy intersected, illuminating the complex challenges of integrating cutting-edge technologies into the time-honored, tradition-steeped landscape of professional sports. This spoke volumes about the evolving nature of sports in the 21st century, marking an era where data, ethics, and performance formed an intricate dance, shaping the future of the game.

The 2016 NBA Finals was a turning point in the acceptance and usage of wearable technology in professional sports. Since then, the impact of these devices has only amplified, revolutionizing various aspects of sports, from training methods and injury prevention to performance optimization and fan engagement. The adoption of wearable technology by athletes, teams, and leagues has changed the game for the better. It has created a new way for athletes to keep performing at their peak and train better. For example, wearable technology gave rise to significant understanding of the following:

- **Improved athlete performance and longevity:** Wearable technology has redefined the contours of athletic performance and longevity. Its advent has facilitated the development of highly individualized training programs that are underpinned by real-time physiological data of athletes. By tracking parameters such as heart rate, acceleration, load, and recovery patterns, these devices empower teams to optimize player performance to ensure that they reach their peak precisely when it is most critical—during high-stakes competitions and playoff games. The benefits of wearable technology are not confined to the court or the field. They also extend into the realm of injury prevention and recovery. With the insights derived from continuous monitoring of biometric data, teams can proactively identify potential injury risks and adjust training regimens accordingly, significantly reducing downtime and ensuring athletes maintain their form for longer periods. This, in essence, has led to extended career spans, a significant boon in the world of professional sports.

- **Advanced injury prevention and recovery:** The impact of wearable technology on injury prevention and recovery protocols has been nothing short of transformative. It has provided coaching staff with the capability to predict and prevent injuries before they happen, a paradigm shift in the management of athlete health. By monitoring metrics such as load, stress, heart rate variability, and sleep patterns, wearables offer a comprehensive overview of an athlete's physical condition. This granular understanding allows the coaching staff to gauge when athletes may be on the brink of an injury, enabling them to tailor training schedules and recovery periods accordingly. Furthermore, when injuries do occur, wearables have proven instrumental in informing recovery protocols. They guide interventions such as rest periods, diet adjustments, and therapy sessions, all of which are tailored based on the athlete's unique physiological data, enabling a safer and more efficient return to play.

- **Greater fan engagement:** In an era of intense competition for viewer attention, wearable technology has presented an innovative avenue for fan engagement. Companies such as WHOOP and Catapult have begun to share anonymized data with broadcasting companies, offering them a unique lens into the performance and condition of athletes. This influx of intricate data has added a new layer of complexity to sports coverage. It has enabled broadcasters to provide viewers with an unprecedented level of insight into the game, enhancing their understanding and appreciation of the strategies, training regimens, and physical prowess of athletes. This depth of coverage has taken fan engagement to new heights, fundamentally altering the sports viewing experience.

- **Enhanced research and understanding:** Lastly, the immense volumes of data generated by wearable technology have proven to be a goldmine for researchers. These data sets have provided scientists with an unprecedented level of insight into athlete health and performance, furthering our understanding of a broad spectrum of topics. Coming from the effectiveness of various training methodologies to the role of sleep and nutrition in athlete performance, these insights are steadily rewriting the playbook of sports science. As such, wearable technology is not just transforming present-day sports, it is also shaping its future, paving the way for new advancements and discoveries that will continue to push the boundaries of athletic performance.

As we look back on the pivotal role of wearable technology in the 2016 NBA Finals, we see more than a landmark event in basketball history; we see the dawn of a new era in sports, an era characterized by an embrace of technological advancements that have had far-reaching impacts on the athletic landscape. Even though the use of wearable technology was prohibited in the official games during the 2016 NBA Finals, the impact that they had during the training sessions led to a monumental change in how the coaches utilized their respective teams during the finals, based on the learnings from this technology.

Wearable technology has indeed heralded a new wave of innovation in sports, driving a paradigm shift in athletic performance optimization. It has done so by delivering a constant stream of comprehensive, real-time physiological data, equipping teams with the critical insights they need to design individualized training programs. These sophisticated regimens allow athletes to reach their performance peaks precisely when it matters the most, shifting the strategic dimensions of professional sports and setting new standards for athletic prowess. Beyond optimizing performance, wearable technology has made substantial strides in enhancing athlete longevity. Through insights that facilitate more effective injury prevention strategies and more sophisticated recovery protocols, athletes can now enjoy longer careers marked by improved health and consistent performance. This revolution in athlete health management is rewriting the conventional wisdom about career lifespans in sports, offering players the opportunity to excel for longer than ever before.

From the standpoint of the millions who watch and love these sports, wearable technology has proved to be a game-changer. It has drastically enriched the viewer experience by integrating detailed performance and biometric data into sports broadcasts. This fusion of technology and sports coverage offers fans a richer, more nuanced understanding of the game, bolstering their engagement and adding a new layer of excitement to sports viewership.

The impact of wearable technology stretches far beyond the court, the field, or the viewers at home. It reaches into the realm of sports science research, where the massive volumes of data generated by these devices offer unprecedented insights into athlete health and performance. These insights are advancing our understanding of a broad array of topics, from training methodologies and techniques to the roles of nutrition and sleep in athlete performance. In this way, wearable technology is not only revolutionizing the present but is also laying the groundwork for the future of sports science.

In the grand scope of sports history, the 2016 NBA Finals stand as a defining moment—a crossroads where tradition met innovation, and the landscape of professional sports began to transform. Wearable technology emerged from this juncture as a powerful tool, influencing every aspect of the game, from athlete performance and career longevity to fan engagement and scientific research.

As we look toward the horizon, envisioning the future of sports, we see a landscape indelibly shaped by the dual forces of wearable technology and data-driven strategies. We see an exciting new era where every leap, every sprint, every swing of the bat is enriched with invaluable data, propelling us further into a realm where athletic potential knows no bounds and the essence of sports science is ceaselessly distilled. In this coming age, the boundaries that once confined our understanding of physical prowess are not merely pushed but shattered. Athletes, armed with real-time insights into their physiological health, can reach new peaks of performance. Coaches, equipped with data never before available, can tailor training regimens with surgical precision, optimizing each individual's capabilities while minimizing the risk of injury.

As we flip the pages of the sports narrative, we see that the chapter of wearable technology is just being penned. This is a narrative imbued with the promise of more groundbreaking discoveries, more awe-inspiring records being toppled, and a deeper reverence for the extraordinary tapestry of human athleticism. Each beep of a heart rate monitor, each flicker on a sleep tracking graph, and each logged recovery period adds to the intricate dance of numbers and performance. These tiny fragments of data come together to compose an intimate portrait of an athlete's journey, adding a whole new layer of understanding and appreciation to the world of sports.

The impact of wearable technology on amateur athletes has been nothing short of transformative. In many ways, this technology has democratized access to advanced sports science, providing individuals at all levels of athletic performance with the tools and insights once reserved for elite professionals.

- **Training optimization:** Wearable devices have provided amateur athletes with valuable insights into their own bodies. These insights can inform a more individualized and effective training regime. For example, heart rate monitors can help athletes identify their optimal training zones for endurance or high-intensity workouts, while sleep trackers can provide guidance on rest and recovery periods.

- **Injury prevention:** Wearable technology has helped amateur athletes better understand their physical limits and risks. By monitoring parameters such as heart rate variability, sleep patterns, and stress levels, athletes can identify signs of overtraining or impending injury. This ability to foresee and mitigate risk can result in fewer injuries, less downtime, and a healthier, more sustainable approach to training.

- **Improved performance:** Wearable technology allows all athletes to monitor and analyze their performance in real time, providing immediate feedback that they can use to adjust their technique or approach. This immediate feedback loop can lead to steady, incremental improvements over time.

- **Healthier lifestyle:** Beyond training and performance, wearable technology has also helped amateur athletes cultivate healthier lifestyles. With features such as sleep tracking, stress monitoring, and activity reminders, wearables can encourage individuals to adopt and maintain habits that support overall well-being, not just athletic performance.

- **Data-driven goals:** Wearables have allowed amateur athletes to set, track, and achieve fitness goals based on quantifiable data. This capacity for objective self-assessment encourages continual progress and can greatly enhance motivation.

The ready access of wearable technology has revolutionized amateur sports by bringing advanced performance metrics and health insights to every individual. These developments have empowered athletes at all levels to train smarter, prevent injuries, improve performance, and live healthier lives. High-tech companies such as Amazon, Apple, Google, and Oura are all getting in on the wearable technology game. They see massive adoption across all types of athletes, from amateur to professional across a wide range of sports.

The technological revolution is not coming; it is here, altering the way we perceive, analyze, and revel in sports. As we move forward, we do so with the exhilaration of knowing that we are part of a thrilling era of discovery, witnessing firsthand the extraordinary ways in which wearable technology is redefining the landscape of sports. This is just the beginning—the prologue to a story that promises to captivate us with each subsequent page turned, each record broken, and each new understanding unearthed. Wearable technology is big business and is growing and getting smarter every day.

The Impact of Live Streaming and Digital Media

The 2017 Invictus Games in Toronto

In the growing shadows of the evening light, the city of Toronto stood poised, a shimmering jewel against the breathtaking backdrop of Canada's expansive landscapes. This wasn't just another evening; the city buzzed with palpable anticipation, a collective heartbeat echoing a singular rhythm of hope and resilience. The evening was alive with promise in the Air Canada Centre, where thousands had gathered excitedly. The venue, usually a battleground for sports teams, was transformed into a grand amphitheater, a sacred ground to honor warriors of a different kind.

As the first notes of music pierced the silence, a dazzling array of lights began to dance, painting stories in hues of gold, blue, and deep scarlet. Projected visuals of rolling oceans and towering mountains filled huge screens, symbolizing the vast challenges the participants had overcome. The sounds and visuals carried tales of valor, of battles fought both on and off the sports fields. Then, the flag bearers entered. Honorably representing 17 nations, they marched in, each step sounding louder with pride and purpose. The flags they bore weren't just pieces of cloth but emblems of countless stories, of sacrifices made and adversities conquered. The Canadian flag, a proud maple leaf, was received with thunderous applause, a testament to the nation's hospitality and the city's enthusiasm.

The 2017 Invictus Games in Toronto had begun, not as a mere sporting event but as a celebration of life, resilience, and the power of the human spirit. The beautiful strains of the nations' national anthems filled the arena, each note a tribute to the unbreakable spirit of the soldiers and veterans whom the Invictus Games honored. As the last notes faded, the stage was graced by performances from Canada's Indigenous dances. Each movement, profound and evocative, paid tribute to the nation's deep-rooted cultural lineage, whispering tales from epochs long past. These ancient narratives wove seamlessly into modern performances, each acting as an ode to unity and the undying flame of the human spirit.

Dignitaries and celebrities, including the founder of the Invictus Games, Prince Harry, stepped onto the stage to address the gathered crowd. Instead of delivering speeches filled with ceremony or pretense, they spoke sincerely from the heart. Their messages were filled with genuine respect, deep admiration, and a true sense of hope for the future and the significance of the occasion. The audience could feel the authenticity and the deep connection the speakers had to the event's purpose and mission. Prince Harry's words echoed a sentiment that formed the foundation of the Invictus Games: "You are proving that anything is possible. You are Invictus."

But perhaps the most impactful moment was when the competitors themselves took center stage. Each face told a story—a story of pain, struggle, but above all, of an unyielding determination. The applause that greeted them wasn't just for their sporting prowess but for their unconquerable souls, their journey from the depths of despair to the pinnacles of triumph. As the ceremony came to a close, a sea of illuminated wristbands glowed in the dark, a beacon of solidarity and support, symbolizing a world united in its admiration for true heroes. The night sky over Toronto was pierced with brilliant fireworks, each explosion a salute to the spirit of the Invictus Games, an ode to those who refused to be defeated.

Throughout the annals of sports, numerous athletes have confronted severe adversities, some grappling with life-altering injuries, others combating profound personal losses. Reflect on the story from the 2017 Invictus Games of Mark Ormrod, a former Royal Marines Commando. After he lost both his legs and his right arm in a landmine explosion in Afghanistan, many would have assumed his athletic days were over. But the call of competition, the allure of the arena was too strong to resist. With unwavering tenacity, Mark transformed his life, and by the time the Invictus Games arrived, he was not just participating but clinching multiple medals in various disciplines, including indoor rowing.

Then there's the inspiring tale of Nerys Pearce, another hero from the 2017 Games. Previously a passionate rugby player, a motorcycle accident left her paralyzed. The shadows of despair might have loomed large, but she found solace in the pool. Swimming became more than a sport to Nerys; it was a therapeutic journey for her. Each stroke in the water was a testament to her resilience, a rhythmic dance that mirrored her inner quest for peace and rejuvenation. At the Invictus Games, her spirit and prowess culminated in a powerful performance, earning her multiple swimming medals and the admiration of countless spectators worldwide.

The Invictus Games—drawing inspiration from the Latin word *invictus*, which translates to "unconquered"—rise as a shining light for the wounded, injured, and ailing members of our military forces. But to view these games as a mere sporting event would be to overlook their profound depth. They are not just about medals or victories on the track; they serve as a powerful emblem of overcoming tremendous odds, a salute to those valiant soldiers and veterans who, while confronting adversaries in battle, also wrestled with the internal struggles that followed their service. Their courage extends beyond the battlegrounds into the arenas of their minds and souls. At the heart of this global phenomenon lies Prince Harry's compassionate vision. Drawing inspiration from the U.S. Warrior Games, he envisaged a platform that would not only celebrate physical prowess but also the indomitable spirit of these heroes. As a result, the Invictus Games emerged as a pulsating movement that has touched every corner of the world. It's a dynamic mosaic, each piece narrating tales of determination, hope, and a relentless drive to reclaim life's purpose. As nations come together, sharing stories of their heroes, the Invictus Games remind us of the universal human spirit that remains unbroken against all odds. Here are the closing lines in Prince Harry's opening speech for the 2017 Invictus Games, which spoke directly to the athletes, the heroes, who were gathered to compete:

> **And now you are here. On the world stage. Flags on your chests. Representing your countries again. Supporting your teammates. And looking up into the stands, and into the eyes of your friends and families. You are all winners. Please don't forget to love every second of it. Don't forget about our friends who didn't come home from the battlefield. Don't forget those at home who still need our support. And don't forget that you are proving to the world that anything is possible. You are Invictus. Let's get started.**

Founded by Prince Harry in 2014, the idea for the Invictus Games was influenced by the Warrior Games in the United States, which the Prince attended in 2013. Prince Harry joked that witnessing the transformative power of sport in accelerating recovery and supporting rehabilitation, the Warrior Games was "such a good idea by the Americans that it had to be stolen." He envisioned a larger, global platform that would bring together competitors from allied nations. Thus, the Invictus Games were born.

The inaugural Invictus Games took place in London in September 2014, seeing participation from more than 400 competitors from 13 countries. Since their inception, the Invictus Games have grown exponentially, both in terms of scale and impact. With each subsequent event, the number of participating nations and competitors has increased, and the games have traveled to various cities worldwide, furthering their mission of fostering hope and rehabilitation.

While the vibrant clashes of athletic competition remain at the heart of the Invictus Games, the deeper essence of these events is far greater than mere physical feats. The Games are not just a platform to showcase strength, agility, or speed. The Games become a transformative journey, a pilgrimage of the soul for many of its participants. For numerous competitors, the road to the Invictus Games is paved with challenges far graver than any sporting rivalry. It is a path of introspection, of confronting and overcoming the haunting memories of battle, the physical scars, and the often more debilitating mental wounds. Engaging in these sports, they don't just chase victory on the field, but a more profound triumph—the restoration of their self-worth that might have been diminished in the aftermath of their injuries or experiences. It's a chance to rekindle a fire within, a spark that perhaps faded in the face of seemingly insurmountable adversities.

As they embark on this transformative journey, the benefits are measured in layers. On the surface, the evident physical recuperation is palpable. Muscles regain their vigor, limbs find their rhythm, and bodies rediscover their former capabilities. But beneath this tangible progress lies the more nuanced psychological healing. The camaraderie of the Games, the shared experiences, and the collective willpower work wonders in alleviating mental anguish, offering solace, and fostering resilience.

Moreover, the broader impact of the Invictus Games stretches beyond the personal growth of the participants. As audiences around the world witness these tales of unparalleled determination, there is a heightened awareness and deepened understanding of the sacrifices that military personnel make. It's a gentle yet powerful reminder of the often-overlooked struggles that these brave souls face, both on the battlefield and in the equally challenging battles that follow their return. In celebrating their spirit, the Games bridge the gap between civilian recognition and military sacrifice, fostering an environment of respect, empathy, and gratitude.

The 2017 Invictus Games in Toronto not only stood as a testament to the undying spirit of wounded warriors but also as a beacon showcasing the profound influence of digital transformation in sports broadcasting. By harnessing the unmatched capabilities of streaming services and digital media platforms, the event achieved unprecedented levels of global accessibility and engagement.

In 2017, the Invictus Games harnessed the burgeoning capabilities of streaming and digital media platforms to broaden their reach and break down traditional viewing barriers. Gone were the days when global events could be accessed only through specific cable channels or exclusive broadcasts. Through platforms such as YouTube, Facebook Live, Instagram, and Periscope (the live-streaming surface provided by X, formerly known as Twitter), coupled with sports-focused streaming sites, the Games opened their doors to global enthusiasts, ensuring that geographic location was no impediment to being part of this extraordinary spectacle. This digital evolution meant that a fan in Sydney, Australia, could be as engrossed in and connected to the action as a local in Toronto, Canada. The Invictus Games became a shining testament to the transformative potential of live streaming in the sports arena.

Live streaming, in essence, is a marriage between the immediacy of traditional broadcasting and the boundless potential of the Internet. It stands as the digital age's answer to our intrinsic desire for real-time experiences, delivering video and audio content directly to our screens with an immediacy that prerecorded content simply can't match. Live streaming captures events as they unfold, allowing viewers to engage with the content spontaneously and without delay.

Unlike the videos we might binge on a lazy afternoon or the podcasts we queue up for a long drive—all of which remain stagnant, waiting for our beck and call—live streams pulse with the heartbeat of the present. They capture the essence of "now," making viewers feel as though they are part of the unfolding narrative, be it a concert, a sporting event, or a news story. While live streaming channels the energy and urgency of traditional media like television or radio, it breaks free from their limitations. Traditional broadcasting is often bound by geographical regions, tethered to specific markets or territories. Live streaming, thanks to the global nature of the Internet, knows no such bounds. Whether you're nestled in a New York apartment, lounging in a cafe in Paris, or trekking through the Himalayas, with a strong enough Internet connection, live streaming ensures that the world's events are but a click away. This democratization of content access not only expands the reach of broadcasts but also fosters a more interconnected global community, united by shared experiences in real time.

The genesis of live streaming is rooted in the early days of the Internet, but its true surge in popularity can be traced back to the late 2000s and early 2010s with the rise of platforms like Justin.tv, which would later evolve into Twitch, and the advent of YouTube's live broadcasting features. Initially, bandwidth limitations and technological constraints posed challenges. However, as technology advanced and Internet speeds accelerated, the potential for high-quality, seamless live streams became a reality. By the time we reached the era of the Invictus Games in Toronto, live streaming had already insinuated itself into the global psyche as a primary mode of content consumption. Traditional broadcasting, while formidable and essential in its heyday, often came with limitations, primarily its geographical boundaries and high operational costs. Live streaming, on the other hand, democratized the playing field.

First and foremost, with live streaming, geographical boundaries were virtually nonexistent. An event taking place in Toronto could be viewed in real time by someone in Tokyo, Cape Town, or Melbourne. This global accessibility meant that events, especially those with universal appeal like the Invictus Games, could resonate with a worldwide audience. Moreover, from a sustainability perspective, live streaming presents a greener alternative to traditional broadcasting. Traditional methods often involve considerable energy consumption with massive broadcasting stations, satellite uplinks, and the infrastructure required to support them. These often lead to higher carbon footprints due to both the energy they consume, and the physical materials required for their construction and maintenance. Contrasting traditional broadcasting, live streaming, with its digital-first approach, minimizes physical infrastructure needs. By leveraging existing Internet networks and data centers, which are continually evolving toward greener operations, live streaming considerably reduces the environmental impact. With fewer on-ground personnel and reduced need for transportation and logistics compared to large broadcasting crews, there's a notable decrease in emissions related to travel and on-site operations.

As streaming technology advances, the equipment needed for streaming is becoming increasingly energy-efficient, and platforms, such as Microsoft Azure, are optimizing data use. This is leading to even lower environmental footprints per broadcast hour. This transition not only represents a win for businesses looking to cut costs but also marks a significant step forward in creating a more sustainable media landscape. While the cost-effectiveness of live streaming is undoubtedly a draw, its lower environmental impact further underscores its advantages, showcasing a harmonious blend of technological progress and environmental responsibility.

Live streaming has truly rewritten the script for audience engagement, merging the barriers between content creators and consumers. Traditional broadcasting, while incredibly effective, often placed the audience in the position of quiet observers, looking into a world where their presence, though appreciated, couldn't directly influence the content being presented. This was a static mode of consumption, where the audience received information without the capacity to reciprocate or converse. However, live streaming has transformed this narrative. With this innovative medium, the passive observer metamorphoses into an active contributor. The interactivity intrinsic to live streaming platforms empowers audiences, allowing their voices to be heard in real time. Whether it's through a live chat, emoji reactions, or even direct video responses on some platforms, viewers have a platform to express their emotions, ask questions, and foster discussions that can be as enriching as the primary content itself.

Imagine a wounded veteran at the 2017 Invictus Games in Toronto, competing and pushing their limits. As they cross a finish line or score a point, not only is the venue alive with applause, but a digital audience worldwide can immediately express their admiration and support. A user in the United Kingdom might send congratulatory messages; another in Brazil might share a similar personal story, forging connections over shared emotions and experiences. These real-time interactions can also provide valuable insights. During the Invictus Games, if an athlete's backstory was shared, a viewer familiar with the tale might add more context or a personal anecdote to the chat, enriching the narrative for all. The same goes for specific rules of a sport or nuances of a particular event. This crowd-sourced knowledge base can significantly enhance the viewing experience.

In essence, the 2017 Invictus Games, when viewed through the lens of live streaming, was not just an athletic event but a global gathering. It was a space where boundaries blurred, stories intertwined, and the collective spirit of humanity was celebrated, with each click, message, and emoji serving as testament to the unifying power of sport and technology. As the Invictus Games in Toronto showcased, live streaming is not just a technological advancement; it's a paradigm shift in how we share and experience collective moments. It's more than a medium; it's a testament to our innate human desire to connect, share, and be part of a global narrative. When paired with the unifying spirit of sports, the power of live streaming can indeed become a beacon of global unity and understanding.

One cannot discuss the evolution of live streaming without addressing its profound impact on advertising and sponsorship opportunities. The traditional broadcasting paradigm relied heavily on fixed commercial breaks, where advertisements were often intrusive and, at times, disjointed from the primary content. Live streaming has offered brands a more organic means of integration. Platforms like Twitch and YouTube have pioneered nonintrusive ad placements, such as banners or sponsored content. This seamless integration ensures that the viewer's experience is not interrupted, while sponsors get the visibility they desire. According to a 2018 report by the Interactive Advertising Bureau, "Live Video Streaming – A Global Perspective," 67 percent of audiences found live stream ads more engaging than on traditional platforms. Combining real-time analytics with live streaming provides advertisers with instantaneous feedback on viewer engagement. Brands can gauge the effectiveness of their messages immediately, allowing for more nimble and responsive marketing strategies. This has attracted a great deal of new sponsors looking to leverage the unique opportunities presented by live streaming.

The 2017 Invictus Games were more than just a display of unparalleled athletic prowess; they became a beacon, illuminating the future of sports marketing in a digital age. As the world tuned in, they weren't merely witnessing the feats of the athletes; they were also observing how brands could form deep, meaningful connections with an expansive global audience.

By attaching their narratives with the Invictus ethos of perseverance, resilience, and victory against odds, sponsors achieved something extraordinary. They shifted from the traditional realm of mere advertising to championing a heartfelt cause. This wasn't the standard brand story being pushed to consumers; it was a genuine two-way conversation. The unique interactivity offered by live streaming platforms—be it instant feedback loops, engaging polls, or dynamic quizzes—allowed brands to tap into the pulse of the audience, adapting their messages and strategies in real-time.

In the vast landscape of this new and exciting digital realm, brands found a wealth of new opportunities to reach their audience. They crafted content that resonated, that viewers sought out not just passively but with an active enthusiasm. The content was shared, tweeted, and discussed, creating ripples across various online platforms. What's more, those once-ignored intermission breaks, previously seen as spaces to momentarily disconnect, now became moments of heightened anticipation. These were the periods where brands, with their tailored content, held the undivided attention of viewers. They became essential to the viewing experience, ensuring that the messages delivered would linger in the minds of the audience long after the Games concluded. The global reach of live streaming meant that geographic borders, which once posed considerable challenges, simply vanished. Sponsors had the golden opportunity to engage not just with a local or national audience but a truly global community. Every like, share, comment, or retweet further expanded their brand's visibility, creating a ripple effect of engagement that traditional broadcasting avenues could only dream of achieving.

Through its pioneering embrace of live streaming and digital engagement, the 2017 Invictus Games showcased the evolving paradigm of sports marketing. It served as a testament to the infinite possibilities that arise when heartwarming, authentic narratives intertwine seamlessly with cutting-edge technology. It laid down a blueprint for how brands can engage—genuinely and profoundly—in the dynamic digital age we find ourselves in.

In the interconnected world of the 21st century, the term *social capital* is more than just another buzzword. It is the glue that binds our social networks, allowing us to build relationships, trust, and cohesiveness in our increasingly fragmented societies. Social capital is, by definition, the network of relationships among people who live and work in a particular society, enabling that society to function effectively. But what does that mean in a tangible sense?

Imagine, for a moment, a vast web of human connections, each thread representing trust, reciprocity, information, and cooperation. These threads, when woven together, create the social fabric of our communities. The strength of this fabric determines the efficiency with which information is shared, resources are mobilized, and common goals are achieved. And in today's age, this tapestry is more diverse and intricate than ever before, spanning cultures, continents, and cyberspaces.

This is the spirit of the Invictus Games. At first glance, it's a platform to recognize the sacrifice and resilience of these brave individuals. But delve deeper, and it becomes evident that the Games serve a much grander purpose—that of fostering social connections, both online and offline. Every participant, every cheer from the stands, every online post shared, is a testament to the power of shared experiences. The Invictus Games bridge the gap between athletes from various backgrounds, experiences, and nationalities, bringing them onto a common platform where camaraderie is celebrated over competition. These connections, forged in the crucible of shared challenges, have a lasting impact, creating ripples in the larger ocean of social interactions. Soldiers from opposite ends of the world find common ground, families share stories of resilience, and communities are reminded of the strength that lies in unity.

Yet, the role of digital media in this context cannot be understated. Today, technology acts as the great equalizer, providing a stage for these shared narratives to be broadcast far and wide. Social platforms amplify the voices of the Invictus Games' participants, allowing even those thousands of miles away to be a part of their journey. Digital media, with its vast reach, breaks down geographical barriers, connecting diverse populations from various countries, backgrounds, and experiences. A tweet from Australia can inspire a tear in England; a photo from Canada can ignite hope in South Africa. It's a symphony of interconnected narratives, each note resonating with the power of the human spirit and shared purpose.

The 2017 Invictus Games, bolstered by the reach of digital media, highlight the essence of social capital in the modern era. They remind us that while individual threads of connection might seem inconsequential when woven together, they create a tapestry of shared experiences and mutual understanding that is truly invincible.

As the world becomes increasingly digital, there are boundless opportunities for sporting events to capitalize on the power of online platforms and technology. By examining trends and observing successful precedents, organizers can significantly increase their reach and impact. We have seen live streaming and the use of digital platforms within sports rise at an extremely fast pace. We can see their impact across a wide variety of events, such as the 2018 Winter Olympics in Pyeongchang, South Korea, offering a stellar example of leveraging digital media for increased impact. To augment its viewership and engage with a global audience, the event was broadcast across various digital platforms, including on the Olympics' official website, on YouTube, and even on social media sites like Facebook and Twitter. Not only did this diversify the audience, but it also allowed for a broader range of content to be shared from interviews and behind-the-scenes clips to instant replays and highlights. The Boston Marathon's adoption of live streaming demonstrates the longevity and scalability of this approach. With the annual race garnering interest from around the world, organizers have continually made use of platforms like Facebook Live, ensuring that fans everywhere can watch the event in real time. This approach isn't just reserved for large-scale events; even smaller tournaments or regional competitions can adopt similar strategies, making it a sustainable choice for events of all magnitudes.

In the rapidly progressing landscape of today's digital age, sporting events are presented with a veritable treasure trove of technological tools and forward-thinking strategies. These innovations, ranging from live streaming to virtual reality, provide a unique opportunity to elevate viewer engagement to unprecedented heights while shattering geographical barriers that once limited an event's reach. The promise is not just in the sheer number of viewers but also in the depth of the experiences crafted for them. By blending the exhilarating highs of sports with cutting-edge technology, organizers can craft moments that linger in memory long after the final whistle has blown.

However, this vast ocean of opportunity also brings with it a necessity for adaptability. As each day sees the advent of new tech advancements, there's an ever-present danger of becoming obsolete. For event organizers, complacency is no longer an option. Continuous learning, experimentation, and a willingness to embrace change are the new norms. Only by doing so can they ensure that they're leveraging the full might of digital advancements, creating sporting spectacles that are not only accessible from any corner of the globe but are also deeply immersive, making every viewer feel like an integral part of the event. In this evolving narrative, it's clear that the fusion of sports and technology heralds a new era of entertainment, one that promises to be as dynamic as it is unforgettable.

The 2017 Invictus Games in Toronto crystallized the transformative role that live streaming and digital platforms play in the contemporary sports landscape. While the athletes' unyielding spirit was undeniably the heart of the event, it was the pioneering use of digital media that amplified their stories to an unparalleled global scale. By harnessing the power of platforms like live streaming, the Games transcended geographical boundaries and brought heartfelt narratives of resilience and triumph to screens worldwide, creating a universal bond of empathy and admiration. In an age where technology often seems to overshadow human endeavors, the Invictus Games turned this narrative on its head. Live streaming and digital platforms were not mere accessories; they became the conduits through which millions felt the pulse of the games, experienced the grit of the participants, and celebrated their victories. This wasn't just about viewing an event; it was about being a part of a global community, connected by the stories that digital media so adeptly shared.

The 2017 Invictus Games stood as a glowing beacon of the unwavering human spirit, and their unparalleled success can be attributed not just to the exceptional athletes but also to the visionary integration of digital innovations. Deeply embedded in the Games was a profound ethos of resilience, recovery, and redefining one's limits. This potent narrative, charged with emotion and determination, was propelled onto a global stage through the dynamic capabilities of live streaming and diverse digital platforms.

Utilizing technology wasn't just a logistical decision; it was a conscious choice to ensure that these stirring tales of heroism, perseverance, and camaraderie resonated with audiences from all corners of the world. Imagine the impact of watching an athlete overcome personal adversities, crossing the finish line, or clinching a victory, and immediately being able to share that experience, discuss it, and celebrate it on platforms like X (formerly known as Twitter), Facebook, YouTube, or Instagram. It created a ripple effect, turning every triumphant moment into a globally shared experience that inspired and connected hearts across continents.The transformative power of these live streaming and digital platforms has significantly reshaped the sporting world as we know it, making it more inclusive and far-reaching than ever before. One of the most significant shifts brought about by this digital revolution is the democratization of access to sports. Gone are the days when international sporting events were restricted to specific cable networks or channels, often unavailable in many regions. Today, platforms such as YouTube, Twitch, and DAZN enable a sports enthusiast in Buenos Aires to seamlessly watch a rugby game unfolding in Auckland or captivate a fan in Mumbai with a live basketball game from Los Angeles.

This new age of broadcasting isn't just more inclusive; it's also more cost-effective. Traditional broadcasting, with its heavy infrastructure and associated costs, often sidelined smaller sports or leagues. However, the advent of digital streaming provides a cost-effective avenue for these sports to reach a global audience, ensuring they no longer remain in the shadows. The interactive nature of these platforms has revolutionized fan engagement. Viewers are no longer passive spectators; they can now engage in real-time chats, participate in instant polls, and share their immediate reactions, making their sports-watching experience richer and more immersive. This interactivity has also paved the way for niche sports, previously overshadowed in their regional confines, to gain global recognition. The power of digital means that sports like Sepak Takraw, primarily known in Southeast Asia, can intrigue viewers in Europe, and sports like Gaelic football can find admirers on distant continents.

The convenience offered by on-demand viewing ensures that fans no longer must be bound by time zones or their schedules. If they miss a live match, they can always catch up at a time that suits them. Coupled with the algorithms that curate content tailored to individual preferences, fans are now getting a more personalized viewing experience, leading to deeper connections with the sports and athletes they love. This digital age doesn't just stop at viewing; it delves deep into the personal stories of athletes often left out of traditional broadcasts. Platforms, especially social media, are instrumental in giving voice to these human-interest tales, enabling fans to forge deeper bonds with their sports heroes and build a global community rooted in mutual respect and admiration.

The vast reach of these digital platforms also translates to lucrative sponsorship opportunities. Brands can now tap into a global audience, aligning with sports and athletes that resonate with a wider demographic. This alignment breaks free from the shackles of geography, opening doors to expansive brand visibility. As technology continues its relentless march forward, the boundaries of sports viewing are being further stretched with the introduction of virtual reality (VR) and augmented reality (AR). These innovations offer fans an unparalleled immersive experience, making them feel as though they are right in the middle of the action, regardless of where they are in the world. The amalgamation of sports with the power of live streaming and digital platforms has ushered in a new era of global sports engagement. It's an era where the thrill of the game is more accessible, experiences are richer, and the bonds between fans and athletes are deeper.

The strategic melding of the Invictus Games' core values with cutting-edge digital technology served as a beacon for other sporting events. It illustrated the profound possibilities that arise when genuine human narratives meet the vast outreach potential of the digital world. As we chart the course for the future of sports and global events, the 2017 Invictus Games stands tall, demonstrating the transformative power of combining authentic stories with technology. Perhaps Prince Harry summed it up best:

And now you are here. On the world stage. Flags on your chests. Representing your countries again. Supporting your teammates. And looking up into the stands, and into the eyes of your friends and families.

You are all winners. Please don't forget to love every second of it. Don't forget about our friends who didn't come home from the battlefield. Don't forget those at home who still need our support. And don't forget that you are proving to the world that anything is possible.

You are Invictus. Let's get started.

Digital Communication as a Catalyst for Peacebuilding

2018 Winter Olympics: Unified Korean Team

In the icy cold of Pyeongchang's wind-swept mountains, a flame began to burn in the winter of 2018—a flame not just from the Olympic torch (a symbol that has united nations and cultures since the times of Ancient Greece) but a flame of hope, unity, and reconciliation between two nations long divided. The Korean Peninsula was a land divided by politics and ideology. In the tremors that followed the conclusion of World War II, the Korean Peninsula found itself partitioned along the 38th parallel. The division of Korea was not a result of the Korean people's wishes; this divide stemmed from the political maneuvering between the Soviet Union and the United States in 1945.

The North fell under Soviet influence, adopting a Communist ideology, while the South aligned with the United States, embracing a capitalist democratic system. The stark ideological divide soon erupted into the Korean War in 1950, a brutal conflict that ended three years later with an armistice agreement but no formal peace treaty. The demilitarized zone (DMZ) was established, a 2.5-mile-wide buffer that separated families, friends, and a people who once shared language, culture, and history.

The division between North Korea and South Korea has since become one of the most enduring and complex geopolitical conflicts of modern times. Attempts at reconciliation have been numerous but often fraught with misunderstandings, mistrust, and external pressures. For more than seven decades, the two nations have seen tensions rise and ebb like the tides of the Han River for more than seven decades. The North and South, separated by a perilous DMZ, have often stood at the brink of hostility, their peoples estranged like families torn apart. But in that winter of 2018, a thaw began to happen. It was a thaw not in the bitterly cold temperatures of the region but in the frosty relations that had long characterized the Korean Peninsula.

Through the power of sports, something extraordinary was about to unfold. The world watched with bated breath as the North Korean and South Korean athletes marched under the unified flag, their faces glowing with a pride that transcended borders and politics. It was a sight that millions around the world had never witnessed. This was a symbol of something greater, something more profound than the united sports team the North Korean and South Korean athletes represented. They symbolized the aspiration for peace and unity that had long been suppressed.

This unprecedented gesture, this unexpected alignment of two worlds, didn't merely emerge out of the thin and frigid air that filled the Olympic stadiums of Pyeongchang. No, it was a masterpiece, carefully and meticulously crafted through the delicate art of diplomacy, woven with threads of patience, understanding, and mutual respect. What set this unique collaboration apart was the innovative use of digital communication. In an age where technology has sometimes become a wedge, a force that divides and isolates, it became, on this momentous occasion, a bridge that connected two disparate worlds.

Leaders from both sides of the Korean divide, aware of the immense weight of history and the watchful eyes of the world, engaged in talks like never before. Their words, once locked behind borders and barriers, were transmitted through screens, devices, satellite signals, traveling over mountains, military lines, and finding their way into the chambers of negotiation. It was a dialogue not only between politicians but between cultures, between philosophies, between the history of a shared past and the promise of a unified future. President Moon Jae-in of South Korea and Supreme Leader Kim Jong Un of North Korea, figures standing at opposite poles of a spectrum, were no longer merely leaders of their respective nations; they were symbols of hopes and dreams, voices representing millions of citizens around the world hoping for peace. Together, they found a common language. This common language wasn't ratified in the cold and sterile corridors of political power. No, it was built in the arena of sports.

The playing fields, where competition, courage, and camaraderie come to life, became the metaphorical meeting ground. They realized that their people, though separated by years of political tension, shared a love for the thrill of the game, the joy of participation, the honor of representing their nation. It was a union that was more than a mere handshake between leaders; it was a handshake between generations. They recognized that their shared Korean heritage and their common love for sports could be a starting point, a spark that could ignite the path toward broader dialogue and reconciliation. Behind closed doors, away from the flashbulbs and headlines, the diplomatic machinery worked tirelessly. Emails were exchanged, video calls were made, documents were drafted and redrafted. Technological innovations, often seen as the tools of the new age, were employed with a sense of purpose and direction, facilitating communication that was not just between governments but between hearts and minds. In the end, the decision to walk together under a unified flag, to compete as one on the icy battlegrounds of Pyeongchang, wasn't just a political maneuver. It was a symbol, a testament to the ability of humankind to overcome even the most profound differences through dialogue, empathy, and the timeless power of sports.

It was a story that demonstrated to the world that in our rapidly evolving digital era, technology could be a force that doesn't just connect devices but connects souls, knitting together a fabric of understanding that can heal wounds and lead to a new future. It was a lesson in humanity that will echo through the passages of time, reminding us that even in our strained and often divided world, we can find common ground if we dare to reach across the divide.

The decision to form a unified women's ice hockey team was a strategic masterstroke, displaying to the world that sport could be a catalyst for peacebuilding. As former UN Secretary-General Ban Ki-moon, himself a South Korean, once observed, "Sport has the power to change the world. It has the power to inspire, it has the power to unite people in a way that little else does."

In a way, the 2018 Winter Olympics became a modern echo of the ancient Olympic truce, where warring city-states laid down arms to engage in peaceful competition. The games became a stage where rivals became teammates, North hugged South, and a puck gliding on ice carried the weight of history and hope.

The global media, often filled with stories of strife and conflict, found in this unified team a narrative of inspiration. It was as if the world needed this story, a reminder that even the most entrenched divisions could be overcome, that humanity could find common ground in the joy and agony of competition. It's a tale of courage, determination, and the timeless human pursuit of harmony, an intricate dance of diplomacy, technology, and sportsmanship that made this remarkable unity possible. In the frosty arenas of Pyeongchang, the 2018 Olympic Games were played, medals were won and lost, anthems were sung, and records were broken. However, beyond the glitz and glamour of the Olympic stage, something more profound had been achieved. A step was taken, a door opened, and a new path explored. The Korean Peninsula and, indeed, the world found in sports a language that speaks of possibilities, dreams, and the undying human spirit. In the words of Pierre de Coubertin, the father of the modern Olympic Games, "The most important thing in the Olympic Games is not winning but taking part; the essential thing in life is not conquering but fighting well." And in the winter of 2018, Korea fought well, not against each other, but together, for a dream that was larger than themselves.

The unified Korean team's story is a lesson in humanity. It's a beacon that shines, telling us that no matter how insurmountable our differences may seem, we can always find a way to the table of brotherhood and peace. It's a legacy that will be cherished, a story that will be told, and a moment that has forever etched itself in the annals of history.

The power of sports as a diplomatic tool has not been lost on the two Koreas. Throughout their troubled history, sports have often served as a platform for tentative gestures of goodwill and attempts at bridge-building. The following are some of the attempts to use sports as the catalyst for unification between the two nations:

- **Seoul Summer Olympics (1988):** A significant early attempt at sports diplomacy was made during the 1988 Summer Olympics in Seoul. Despite extensive negotiations, the two sides were unable to agree on the details of a unified participation. North Korea, feeling slighted, boycotted the games.

- **Ping-Pong diplomacy (1991):** A more successful endeavor came in the form of table tennis when the two Koreas formed a joint team for the World Table Tennis Championships in 1991. This collaboration marked the first unified Korean team since the division and symbolized a temporary thaw in relations.

- **Sydney Summer Olympics (2000):** The world witnessed another monumental moment when athletes from North Korea and South Korea marched together under a unified flag during the opening ceremony of the 2000 Sydney Olympics. Though they competed separately, the act was an impactful gesture and laid the ground-work for future collaborations.

- **Inter-Korean Soccer Matches:** Over the years, soccer matches between North Korea and South Korea have provided sporadic opportunities for interaction. These games, often charged with political undercurrents, have been symbolic encounters reflecting the broader relationship between the two nations.

The history of sports diplomacy between North Korea and South Korea is a complex tableau littered with political, cultural, and historical threads. Each attempt has been a dance between hope and the harsh reality of two worlds so ideologically divided and a reflection of the broader desire for reconciliation. In the shadow of their divided past, sports have offered a rare space where the two Koreas could explore shared identity and common humanity. Not all attempts have been successful, but each has added a layer to an ever-evolving relationship, a relationship that found its most powerful layer to date in the 2018 Winter Olympics and a truly unified Korean team.

The journey toward the unified Korean team represents more than a passing footnote in the annals of sports history; it was a landmark moment that cut across the boundaries of sports and touched the very soul of humanity. It was a reminder that even throughout decades of division, common ground can be found and bridges can be built. It was a testament to the power of vision, dialogue, and collaboration. It was a symbol of what is possible when we dare to dream, when we have the courage to reach across the divides that separate us. The unified Korean team at the 2018 Winter Olympics eclipsed being merely a team; it was a movement, a powerful global message, a symphony of hope that still echoes, still inspires, and still reminds us of the profound and beautiful potential that lies within us all.

It was a groundbreaking journey that began in 2017, which led toward the unified Korean team for the 2018 Winter Olympics, a journey that defied decades of division, conflict, and mistrust, and culminated in a moment that reverberated around the world. In 2017, the Korean Peninsula was a tinderbox of escalating tensions. The worrying nuclear tests in the North were met with international condemnation, and missile launches traced arcs of global anxiety across the skies. A cloud of uncertainty hovered, with world leaders and common citizens alike holding their breath, caught in a relentless cycle of provocations and reprisals. Amid this volatile backdrop, the most unexpected of conversations began. Into this complex political situation stepped South Korea's newly elected President Moon Jae-in, a man whose name would become synonymous with peaceful engagement. A veteran of inter-Korean relations and a proponent of dialogue, President Moon was acutely aware of the delicate threads that held the peace.

In June 2017, with the 2018 Winter Olympics on the horizon, President Moon extended an olive branch that was as unexpected as it was profound. He proposed that the two Koreas "march together during the Asian Winter Games."

The symbolism of this gesture cannot be overstated. Marching together, two Koreas that had been torn apart, whose history was marred by war and division, was a vision that far exceeded mere politics. It was a message of hope, a bold stroke of diplomacy that sought to turn the page on a dark chapter and welcome in a new, brighter future for both nations. The North remained silent initially, a silence that was both enigmatic and tense. Was this an outright rejection or a moment of contemplation? The world watched, and the speculation grew. Months passed until finally, as the world welcomed a new year, Kim Jong Un, the Supreme Leader of North Korea, broke the silence. In his 2018 New Year's speech, he signaled an openness to the idea, a subtle but significant shift. He expressed a desire for an easing of tension between the two nations and said that the North would be "prepared to take various steps, including the dispatch of the delegation." The words were measured, but the implications were vast. Was this the dawn of a new era, or a fleeting moment of détente? The whispers of hope grew louder, and the International Olympic Committee (IOC) emerged as the catalyst. Recognizing the historic opportunity, the IOC played a key role in facilitating the talks, working closely with both sides to create an environment conducive to collaboration.

The negotiations were intricate, laden with historical baggage and geopolitical complexity. The IOC's involvement was rooted in its core principles, as outlined in the Olympic Charter. The charter calls for "promoting a peaceful society concerning human dignity" and "to place sport at the service of humanity" (Olympic Charter, Rule 2). These principles provided the philosophical underpinning for the IOC's engagement with the two Koreas. One key individual from the IOC who made the impossible thought of a unified Korean team a reality was IOC president, Thomas Bach. He was a central figure in the organization's efforts. A former Olympic fencer, Bach's leadership was characterized by a blend of determination and diplomacy. He was quoted as saying, "The Olympic Games are always about building bridges; they never erect walls." His vision was instrumental in turning the idea of a unified team from dream to reality. Another key IOC figure was Christophe Dubi, the Olympic Games executive director; he played a vital role in coordinating the logistics and ensuring that the unified team's participation met all the necessary Olympic criteria.

The creation of the unified Korean team for the 2018 Winter Olympics was a complex process, involving many key figures from various domains, including political leaders, sports authorities, and international bodies. These key figures facilitated numerous rounds of talks between the North and South, which culminated in the historical "Olympic Korean Peninsula Declaration," an agreement that outlined the terms of the unified team's participation ahead of the 2018 Winter Olympics. This declaration laid the groundwork for a series of unprecedented cooperative measures, including the joint marching of the two nations under a single flag during the opening ceremony. The key provisions of this agreement included the following:

- **Unified participation:** The two Koreas would march together under a unified flag depicting the Korean Peninsula during the opening ceremony.

- **Unified women's ice hockey team:** North and South Korea agreed to form a joint women's ice hockey team, making it the first unified Korean team in Olympic history.

- **Cultural performances:** The agreement also included provisions for joint cultural performances, promoting a sense of shared cultural heritage.

The path to this agreement, with all its twists and turns, could rival a Hollywood blockbuster. It began with the initial seeds of diplomacy, planted by President Moon's proposals, and was nurtured by Kim Jong Un's positive response, growing into an unprecedented alliance that captured the world's attention. Both countries engaged in high-level talks at the Peace House in the DMZ. These talks involved key representatives from both North Korea and South Korea. The IOC, under Bach, played a vital role in mediating and facilitating the negotiations. A four-party meeting involving the IOC, North Korea, South Korea, and the PyeongChang Organizing Committee led to the final agreement, which balanced the interests of both Koreas to ensure compliance with Olympic rules and principles.

The Olympic Korean Peninsula Declaration stands as a symbol of how sports can transcend political and ideological barriers. It provided a rare moment of unity and cooperation between the two Koreas, casting aside decades of division and mistrust. The successful implementation of the agreement during the 2018 Winter Olympics sent a powerful message to the world about the potential of dialogue, empathy, and the unifying spirit of sportsmanship. It wasn't merely a sports pact; it was a beacon of hope for a region fraught with tensions and, indeed, for a world in need of peace and understanding.

In the unique and sensitive context of inter-Korean relations surrounding the 2018 Olympics Games, the role of digital communication— the transmission of information between two or more parties using electronic technologies—stood out as the game changer, surpassing conventional means of diplomacy, and took on a defining character in shaping the unified Korean Olympic team. Digital communication encompasses various means such as emails, videoconferencing, secure messaging, and direct hotlines. These channels allow secure and private real-time interaction, documentation, and collaboration across geographical and political boundaries.

The Korean Peninsula, divided since the armistice of 1953, has been characterized by mistrust, political tension, and limited interaction. Traditional means of communication had been cumbersome and hampered greatly by diplomatic barriers. Against this backdrop, digital communication emerged as an essential bridge between the two nations, enabling a level of engagement that had not been seen before. The use of digital communication was key in the negotiations that led to the unified Korean Olympic team. It wasn't just about exchanging information; it was about making connections. North Korean and South Korean officials were able to engage with each other as individuals, not just as representatives of opposing governments. This direct and personal interaction added a new level of understanding and cooperation to the talks. It made the process more immediate, nuanced, and personal. What was achieved went beyond the realm of sports. It touched on deeper themes of shared identity, peace, and reconciliation.

The first order of business was the reactivation of the hotline between Seoul and Pyongyang, which was a seminal moment for the negotiations. This telephone line was a symbol of direct dialogue and a commitment from both sides to break down decades of silence. The hotline, previously cut off due to rising tensions, became the first channel through which both sides could communicate quickly and candidly. In a landscape where every word was weighted with historical significance, the hotline allowed for swift decisions, bypassing the usual diplomatic red tape and the ever-present public eye. It served as a permanent olive branch, reconnecting two nations that had been estranged for far too long.

The utilization of videoconferencing platforms facilitated face-to-face interactions between officials from both North Korea and South Korea. In an environment where trust was in short supply, the visual connection allowed the negotiators to observe each other's facial expressions and body language. These nonverbal cues humanized the interactions, turning abstract negotiations into personal connections. It transformed sterile political discourse into a living dialogue, building rapport and trust that would have been unthinkable through traditional communication channels.

The negotiations were characterized by a dense web of proposals, counterproposals, agreements, and revisions. Applications like Microsoft Outlook and secure messaging apps enabled the continuous exchange of these crucial documents. The real-time collaboration was vital to keeping both sides on the same page and ensuring that the IOC was synchronized with the efforts from both Korean leaders. In the frantic pace leading up to the Olympics, these tools streamlined the communication process, transforming what could have been a logistical nightmare into a coherent and coordinated effort.

In the delicate negotiations that led to the creation of the unified Korean Olympic team, security and confidentiality were not mere considerations but essential foundations. This was not simply a conversation between athletes or sporting bodies; it was a discussion that had the potential to reshape the political landscape of the Korean Peninsula. The use of encrypted communication channels, such as those often facilitated through Secure Sockets Layer (SSL) technology, was key for ensuring this security. These protocols go beyond simple password protection, encrypting data so that it would remain unintelligible even if intercepted without unintelligible without the specific decryption keys.

The importance of using such secure channels was twofold. First, it underscored the seriousness of the negotiations. Both sides knew that the stakes were high and that any leak or breach could derail the entire process. By employing advanced encryption and other security measures, they were signaling to each other that they were committed to a process that was fair, transparent, and immune to outside interference. Second, the security measures were about building trust. For the North Korean and South Korean officials, establishing a line of communication that was impenetrable to outside eyes allowed them to speak more openly and candidly. They knew their words would not be taken out of context or used against them. It allowed them to explore options and express opinions that might have been too risky in a less secure environment.

In addition to SSL, the use of virtual private networks (VPNs) to create secure connections over the public Internet and two-factor authentication (2FA) tokens for additional layers of security would protect not only the content of the communications but also the identity of the participants. Beyond the encryption and authentication, monitoring and regular security audits ensured that the systems were not compromised. Regular updates and patching of the software ensured that no known vulnerabilities were left open to exploitation.

In the world of diplomacy, where words can be as powerful as actions, the security of the communication channels represented far more than a simple technical checkmark; it was a symbolic act. It reflected the commitment of both parties to a dialogue that was honest, respectful, and private. The role of technology in ensuring this security was vital. It allowed two nations, long estranged and deeply mistrustful of each other, to come together in a space that was both virtual and yet intensely real. It provided a forum where they could speak not only as representatives of different governments but as individuals striving for a common goal. The creation of the unified Korean Olympic team will be remembered for the athletes' performances, but it will also be remembered for the way technology bridged a divide that had seemed unbridgeable. The digital tools that enabled this connection were not mere bytes and bits but forged from trust, respect, and a shared vision of peace. And at the heart of this connection was the understanding that security was central in allowing two rival nations to speak to each other with confidence and hope.

The clicks, dials, and video calls were not mere transactions but bridges, turning distance into proximity, suspicion into trust, and impossibility into reality. It's a powerful example that speaks to the power of digital connection in a divided world, a lesson that resonates far beyond the arena of sports. In creating the unified Korean Olympic team, digital communication was more than a collection of tools; it was a dynamic ecosystem that shaped the dialogue and influenced outcomes. It broke down barriers, fostered empathy, and provided a framework within which complex negotiations could unfold. The process was no longer confined to cold, formal interactions but became a living dialogue marked by humanity, cooperation, and a shared vision. The historical weight of the division was momentarily lifted, replaced by a sense of connection, possibility, and hope, all enabled by the quiet revolution of digital communication. In this way, technology not only served diplomacy but elevated it to a new plane of understanding and common purpose. It's a narrative that resonates far beyond the Korean Peninsula, offering insights into how digital diplomacy can redefine international relations in the 21st century.

In an age marked by the rapid flow of information and instant connectivity, the 2018 Olympic Games in Pyeongchang presented an extraordinary example of how digital communications could forge connections across continents and cultures. Outside of the delicate diplomatic digital dialogues that came together to find common ground and establish the historic first unified Korean Olympic team, a parallel narrative emerged: the role of digital communication in sharing the splendor, emotion, and narratives of these Games with a global audience. The digital communication in the 2018 Winter Olympics extended beyond the corridors of diplomacy into the hearts and screens of people worldwide. The Games were no longer confined to the arenas in Pyeongchang. They came alive in the virtual spaces where fans lived, worked, and gathered. Social media became the modern town square, where stories were told and retold, voices were heard, and connections were made. The unified Korean Olympic team's story, emblematic of what sports can achieve, was narrated, celebrated, and relived through these digital channels, making the 2018 Winter Olympics a truly global and timeless experience. Social media platforms were not merely tools or channels; they were the arteries through which the pulse of the Games was felt across the world. Through Twitter, Facebook, Instagram, YouTube, and even emerging platforms, billions had access to an Olympic experience like never before.

The immediacy and reach of Twitter turned it into a real-time commentary box, a global gathering spot where moments were shared the instant they occurred. Tweets from world leaders, athletes, celebrities, and ordinary fans mingled to create a rich tapestry of reactions and emotions. In the world of social media, hashtags often serve to categorize content or promote trending events. They can come and go with fleeting attention. Yet, #KoreaUnification stood apart from typical trends. It emerged as a digital banner under which people from different nations, cultures, and political ideologies could stand together. The hashtag #KoreaUnification became a rallying cry, a symbol of hope that rose to be as important as the Games themselves. The hashtag did not only represent the enormity of North Korea and South Korea fielding a unified team. It was so much more than the specifics of sports, embodying a yearning for peace and reconciliation that was deeply resonant. For Koreans on both sides of the border and the Korean diaspora worldwide, it invoked a sense of national identity, a shared history, and a hope for a future without division. #KoreaUnification was actively used by politicians, celebrities, athletes, and ordinary people to express support for the idea of unity. The hashtag was shared on various platforms, making it a common thread that connected different narratives, images, and voices. It allowed individuals to feel part of a larger community, rallying around a common cause. Unlike many trending hashtags that fade away after the event, #KoreaUnification left an enduring legacy. It continues to be referenced in discussions about inter-Korean relations and is often cited in academic papers, news articles, and political discourses as a poignant moment of digital diplomacy. Its resonance extends beyond the temporal boundaries of the Games, serving as a historical marker of a time when sports, politics, and digital communication converged to touch hearts and minds globally. The unified Korean team sparked an unprecedented digital movement with online campaigns, petitions, and global solidarity movements. The hashtag #KoreaUnification became a viral trend, resulting in a global cry for peace, mobilizing support from various corners of the world. Petitions on platforms like Change.org were initiated, urging continuous dialogue and peace talks between the two nations.

As the world's most extensive social network at the time, Facebook's role in disseminating stories, videos, and photographs was unparalleled. Long-form articles analyzing the significance of the unified team, live streams of the events, and poignant images of North Korean and South Korean athletes smiling together were shared across continents, initiating dialogues and debates that enriched the collective understanding of what the 2018 Games represented. The platform also became a place for in-depth analysis and thoughtful commentary. Journalists, scholars, and commentators provided long-form articles that delved into the historical significance of the unified team, the diplomatic nuances, and the broader implications for peace and cooperation. These articles helped to contextualize the event, providing layers of understanding that went beyond mere spectacle. Facebook's global reach meant that conversations about the unified team were not confined to any specific region or community. People from different countries, cultures, and political backgrounds engaged in dialogues and debates. The platform allowed for a diversity of perspectives, and the comment sections often turned into lively forums for discussion. This multitude of voices added depth and complexity to the narrative, reflecting the multifaceted nature of the event itself. Facebook's role in the 2018 Winter Olympics was about more than information dissemination; it was about creating a rich, interconnected tapestry of engagement that brought the world closer to the Games and to the profound story of the unified Korean team. Its multifaceted approach—combining visual storytelling, analytical insight, real-time engagement, and community building—offered a comprehensive and deeply human perspective on an event that was more than just sports; it was a moment of historical, political, and cultural significance that continues to resonate.

YouTube, a central hub for video content, emerged as a significant platform for showcasing the journey of the unified Korean team during the 2018 Winter Olympics. From heart-stirring highlights and thought-provoking interviews to in-depth analyses and comprehensive documentaries, YouTube played an instrumental role in chronicling the pivotal moments that marked these Olympics. What made this platform even more remarkable was its accessibility. Available to anyone with an Internet connection, the visual narratives on YouTube served as timeless monuments, capturing, and immortalizing the spirit, triumphs, and tribulations of the Games.

However, YouTube wasn't alone in this endeavor. The 2018 Winter Olympics signaled a watershed moment for streaming, with a host of streaming services stepping up to the plate. YouTube TV, Hulu, Roku, Sling, and Apple TV, among others, not only offered an abundance of options but also confirmed that streaming was no longer a fledgling technology; it was a robust and viable medium, marking a new era in how the world consumed sports. NBC, long regarded as the home of the televised Olympics, also adapted to this changing landscape. It rolled out the NBC Olympics app, providing audiences an enriched and interactive experience. The app wasn't merely a gateway to live streams; it was a comprehensive portal that included replays, expert commentary, nuanced analysis, and a treasure trove of content that allowed viewers to delve deeper into the Games. The convergence of these platforms, each with its unique offerings, painted a vibrant and multifaceted picture of the Olympics. Whether it was the emotional roller coaster of the unified Korean team's journey or the technical mastery of individual athletes, these digital avenues provided a window into the very soul of the Games. This wasn't just about viewing; it was about engaging, understanding, and becoming part of a global community that celebrated human endeavor, unity, and the power of sports to ignore barriers. In a world that often seemed fragmented and polarized, the 2018 Winter Olympics, aided by platforms like YouTube and NBC's app, served as a beacon, reminding us of our shared humanity and the potential for connection, empathy, and understanding. It was a testament to the ongoing evolution of technology and its ability to bring the world closer, one stream, one highlight, one story at a time.

Digital diplomacy emerged as an essential aspect of maintaining momentum in inter-Korean relations following the Olympic Games.

Analyzing conversations across various online platforms, including social media and official government channels, reveals a strategic use of digital technology to maintain dialogue. These digital channels allowed for private and semipublic back-channel discussions, allowing North Korean and South Korean officials to negotiate in a more fluid, adaptable environment. This was crucial in keeping communication channels open and enabling real-time interactions, minimizing misunderstandings, and promoting trust. The digital sphere provided a platform where supportive voices from around the world could converge, reinforcing international approval and encouraging positive negotiations. This digital footprint, filled with opinions, analyses, and expectations, became part of the broader diplomatic landscape, reflecting the global consensus toward peace and unity. Digital platforms proved to be more than just tools for conversation; they became enablers of continued dialogue. The accessibility and ubiquity of these platforms allowed not only government officials but also ordinary citizens to partake in a global conversation about Korean unity. Social media campaigns, online petitions, virtual summits, and discussion forums kept the spirit of the unified Korean team alive. These platforms allowed for a nuanced exploration of common cultural heritage, shared experiences, and hopes for a peaceful future, thus humanizing the diplomatic process and making it more transparent and inclusive. In this age of connectivity, digital platforms have become vital diplomatic instruments that foster continuous dialogue and engagement beyond formal channels.

The sports diplomacy initiated by the unified Korean team didn't end with the closing ceremony of the Winter Olympics. Several post-Olympics sporting events carried on this legacy, with combined North Korean and South Korean teams participating in various competitions and friendly matches. These events were televised and streamed online, keeping the global audience engaged. Each game was more than a sporting competition; it symbolized cooperation, friendship, and shared goals. The continued collaboration in the sporting arena was a tangible sign that the spirit of unity was more than a temporary show; it had become a sustainable movement. The synergy between sports and digital diplomacy demonstrates a promising avenue for future peacebuilding initiatives. The potential to use sports as a recurring diplomatic tool, supported and magnified by digital communication, has been proven to be an effective strategy. Whether through live streaming, social media engagement, or digital storytelling, technology can elevate the impact of sports diplomacy. It bridges geographical distances, engages diverse demographics, and fosters a shared experience. Going forward, nations can explore this synergy in various diplomatic contexts, not only to solve conflicts but also to build lasting relationships. By embracing sports, a universal language of humanity, and coupling it with the far-reaching impact of digital communication, governments, organizations, and communities can work toward a more harmonious and interconnected world.

The historic events of 2018, culminating in the unified Korean team at the Winter Olympics, showcased an innovative intersection of sports and digital diplomacy. This collaboration offers a new model of international relations that is more inclusive and dynamic and that resonates strongly with the global community. It's a testament to the power of human connection and shared values, enhanced and enabled by technology. The stories, interviews, and sound bites from North Korean and South Korean athletes offered a personal and human perspective that connected with people on a profound level. The athletes were no longer abstract representatives of conflicting ideologies; they were individuals with dreams, emotions, and aspirations. Ryu Seung-min, a South Korean Olympic table tennis champion, voiced his joy at shaking hands with North Korean players, stating, "They are not the enemy; they are partners for the unification."

The conversations did not end with the closing ceremony. Digital platforms continued to buzz with discussions, analyses, and reflections on the unification prospects. From scholarly articles to opinion pieces in digital media, the narrative transitioned from sports diplomacy to a broader discourse on peace, reconciliation, and the potential roadmap toward unification. The image of athletes from North Korea and South Korea marching under a single Korean Peninsula flag during the opening ceremony is a moment that resonated across the world. The unity displayed was more than a symbol; it was a tangible demonstration of a shared identity that held no regard for political boundaries. The photograph of this unprecedented march was shared and commented upon widely, becoming an emblem of hope and reconciliation. It's a moment etched in history, starkly contrasting the militarized border that separates the two nations. The extraordinary journey of the unified Korean team at the 2018 Winter Olympics is a multifaceted tale that exemplifies the confluence of history, sports, diplomacy, and the revolutionary impact of digital communication. It was a moment where technology outshone its functional role to become an instrument of peace, human connection, and global engagement. Digital platforms allowed us to witness, in real time, the transformation of a deeply divided peninsula into a symbol of unity. The social media buzz, live streams, and online campaigns were not mere appendages to the event; they were the channels through which a world, often fragmented by differences, found common ground in the universal language of sports and the shared human values of empathy, understanding, and reconciliation. In a delicate geopolitical landscape, digital communication acted as both a catalyst and a chronicler, enabling discreet negotiations behind the scenes and capturing the poignant public moments that defined these Games.

In reflecting upon the journey of the unified Korean team during the 2018 Winter Olympics and the digital wave that followed, it becomes crystal clear that sports have a transformative power that pays no mind to borders, politics, and historical grievances. The extraordinary events of the 2018 Olympics, both on the field and within the digital landscape, have left a lasting imprint, marking a pivotal moment in inter-Korean relations and global diplomacy. The shared march under the Korean Peninsula flag, the ensuing online conversations, and the post-Olympic sporting events that continued the legacy of unity were not mere symbolic gestures; they became the embodiment of cooperation, friendship, and a shared vision for peace. Through digital diplomacy, back-channel discussions were analyzed, negotiations were fostered, and continuous dialogue was enabled between the North and South. This symbiosis of sports and technology, personified in the unified Korean team, has ushered in a new era of diplomatic synergy.

What makes the 2018 Winter Olympics an emblematic milestone is not confined to the spectacle of sports itself but to the intertwining of the human spirit with technological advancement. Digital platforms amplified the voices calling for peace, unity, and understanding, broadening the reach of these messages to corners of the world otherwise untouched by diplomatic channels. Online communities and forums became breeding grounds for empathy and shared human aspiration, reinforcing the global push toward reconciliation. The lasting digital footprints of this historical moment are a testament to the potential of sports to bridge divides, the power of digital media to amplify voices, and the enduring human aspiration for peace and unity. In the annals of history, the 2018 Olympics will be remembered not just for the medals won or records broken but for the pioneering way in which technology and the human spirit converged to craft a narrative that resonated across boundaries and generations. The fusion of sports and digital communication, as witnessed in the 2018 Winter Olympics, illuminates a path forward for Korea as well as for the global community. It is a beautiful reminder that the arenas of competition can become theaters of change and that our collective drive for excellence, understanding, and peace can forge connections that reshape our world.

Creating an Inclusive and Accessible Fan Experience

2018 FIFA World Cup: France's Victory

The Luzhniki Stadium in Moscow was the epicenter of excitement and anticipation as the world gathered for the opening of the 2018 FIFA World Cup. The stadium was filled to capacity with fans from every corner of the globe. Flags of various nations were prominently displayed, each one representing the pride and unity of its people. The breeze gave life to the colors, creating a visual representation of the global community that had come together for this event.

The opening ceremony began with precision and grandeur. Dancers dressed in traditional Russian costumes took to the stage, performing routines that showcased Russia's diverse cultural heritage. Their movements were well-rehearsed and elegant, reflecting the country's history and traditions. Musicians played traditional instruments including the balalaika (a guitar-like instrument) and Tatar drums, producing sounds that were distinctly Russian. The music was neither overly dramatic nor subdued; it was a fitting accompaniment to the visual spectacle resonating with the audience and creating a connection between the performers and the audience.

The ceremony was more than just a prelude to a sporting event; it was a carefully orchestrated celebration of humanity. It acknowledged the power of football to bring people together, regardless of their differences. The performers, the music, and the overall ambiance were carefully chosen to represent the host country as well as the global football community. Russia, with its complex history and diverse landscape, was the host of the 2018 FIFA World Cup. The country's contradictions and contrasts were subtly reflected in the ceremony, hinting at the complexity of the nation and its people. The event was a testament to the ability of sport to bridge cultural divides and foster mutual understanding. The crowd's reaction was enthusiastic but measured. Fans cheered, clapped, and expressed their approval, but there was also a sense of contemplation and appreciation for the deeper message of the ceremony. The excitement for the upcoming matches was palpable, but so was the recognition of the unifying power of the game. As the ceremony concluded, the focus shifted to the tournament itself. The stage was set, the teams were ready, and the world was watching. The 2018 FIFA World Cup was not only about competition and victory; it was about collaboration, respect, and the shared love for the game. On that memorable day, Luzhniki Stadium was a symbol of what football can achieve. It was a reminder that the sport is more than just a game. It's a global language that speaks to the hearts of billions. It's a platform that transcends boundaries, celebrates diversity, and unites people in a common goal.

As the fireworks lit up the Moscow sky in celebration, another narrative was taking shape—a narrative of innovation, evolution, and the relentless march of progress. The game had come a long way since the sun-kissed World Cup days of Brazil in 2014. Technology, once a peripheral presence, had become a central character in the drama of football. As you saw in Chapter 2, the 2014 FIFA World Cup in Brazil was a vibrant showcase of football, yet it was a tournament where technology played a supporting role rather than a starring one. While there were examples of fantastic technological innovation, such as the rise and adoption of data science to help create better outcomes, its impact on the fan experience was relatively limited.

Fast-forward to the 2018 FIFA World Cup in Russia, and the landscape had transformed dramatically. The triumph of technology was not merely a subplot; it was a defining narrative that reshaped the game and enriched the fan experience. One of the most significant advancements was the implementation of the video assistant referee (VAR) system. The 2014 World Cup was marred by controversial decisions and human errors, but in 2018 VAR brought a new level of transparency and fairness. Fans were no longer passive spectators; they were engaged participants, analyzing the same replays that the referees were examining and being given insights into the rationale behind critical decisions.

The 2018 World Cup also saw the rise of digital platforms that democratized access to the game. While the 2014 tournament relied heavily on traditional broadcasting, 2018 embraced streaming services, social media, and interactive apps. Fans from remote villages to bustling cities could connect, share, and celebrate the game in real time. The barriers of geography and socio-economic status were eroded, creating a truly global and inclusive community. The World Cup was a celebration of connectivity, engagement, and community. The rise of digital platforms redefined the fan experience, transforming it from a solitary act of watching to a communal act of sharing, connecting, and belonging. It was a testament to the power of technology and its ability to entertain but also enlighten, empower, and unite. It was a glimpse into a future where the beautiful game is truly the game of the world, accessible to all, and cherished by all.

Furthermore, the use of augmented reality (AR) and virtual reality (VR) in 2018 provided fans with immersive experiences that were unthinkable in the previous World Cup. Whether it was virtual stadium tours or AR-enhanced match statistics, fans were transported into the heart of the action, bridging the gap between the physical and digital worlds. The contrast between 2014 and 2018 is a testament to the rapid evolution of technology and its profound impact on the sport. It's a journey from tentative exploration to confident embrace, from isolated innovation to holistic integration. The 2018 World Cup was a celebration of football; it was a celebration of progress, inclusivity, and the unifying power of technology. It was a glimpse into the future of the beautiful game, where fans are not mere spectators but active participants in a global community.

As the players took to the pitch, their every move tracked by cameras and algorithms, it was clear that this was a new era. The lines between the physical and digital were blurred, and the roar of the crowd was amplified by the clicks and tweets of a global audience. The opening ceremony was a perfect showcase of this transformation. A blend of art and science, emotion and logic, human skill and technological power. It was a glimpse into a future where football was not just a game but an intersection of culture, technology, and passion, as well as a showcase for a game so loved by billions of fans across the world.

The digital age has played a major role in shifting the landscape around player tracking systems; it has reconstructed it. From rudimentary pedometers and basic GPS technologies that hinted at the future back in the early 2000s, we've catapulted into an era where player tracking is the beating heart of a transformative shift. As described in Chapter 2, firms like STATSports and Catapult Sports, which once existed on the periphery as gleams in the eyes of future-thinkers, have now solidified their roles as the cornerstones of modern sports analytics. Don't be fooled, though. These tracking systems extend beyond simple "fittech"—they've become the digital extensions of coaching staff. Coaches are now armed with an array of metrics so expansive and intricate that it alters the very architecture of player development and strategic thinking.

Metrics covering speed, stamina, heart rate, and even layers of complexity like expected goal value (or xG as it's commonly known), is one of the most riveting and insightful metrics in modern football analytics. Imagine xG as a crystal ball, not perfect but incredibly adept at predicting the probability of a shot resulting in a goal based on various factors. Let's set the scene: A striker is rushing toward the goal, the angle is tight, defenders are closing in, and he's using his weaker foot. Traditional stats might simply log this as a "shot on target" if it doesn't find the net, but xG delves deeper. Expected goal value assigns a numerical value between 0 and 1 to each shot taken, calculated based on myriad variables such as distance from the goal, angle to the goal, player position, the part of the body used, defensive pressure, and even historical data on how similar shots have fared in the past. It provides a great deal of information, far more detailed than that of a typical snapshot; it's more like a short film that considers the context of the play. A shot with an xG of 0.3, for instance, would be expected to result in a goal 30 percent of the time under similar circumstances. It's this depth that makes xG an invaluable tool for coaches, analysts, and even fans.

In the context of player tracking systems, xG becomes even more potent. Pair it with real-time data on player speed, positioning, and stamina, and you get an evolving tactical map. Coaches can identify who's making the runs and taking the shots but they are also able to pinpoint who's doing so in the most dangerous and effective ways. Likewise, fans armed with xG data during live broadcasts can have deeper, more nuanced conversations and understand the game in ways previously reserved for professionals. So, when we talk about complex layers like expected goal value, we're looking at a metric that synthesizes multiple elements of the game into a singular, easily digestible figure. It democratizes understanding and raises the bar of strategy, making it an essential aspect of the fascinating interplay between technology and the age-old beautiful game. This arsenal of data allows for an almost granular dissection of each player's performance, setting the stage for strategic decisions that are so hyper-focused and individualized, they can dictate the outcome of a match in real time.

When it came to implementing player tracking systems, the French Football Federation left no stone unturned. It partnered with companies renowned for their sports analytics' solutions to arm manager Didier Deschamps and his staff with an array of high-definition, real-time data. This wasn't merely about keeping tabs on player movement; it was about distilling that movement into actionable insights.

Consider the iconic speed on the pitch demonstrated by Kylian Mbappé, France's dynamic forward. It's one thing to note that Mbappé is fast; it's another to realize, based on data from tracking systems, that his peak acceleration often occurs during specific phases of the game or against certain defensive setups. This level of insight, derived from metrics that capture every sprint, turn, and touch, gave the French team a sort of "sixth sense." It provided them with the ability to strategize around the unique strengths and limitations of their players, and also those of their opponents.

And then there's N'Golo Kanté, the tireless midfielder on the French squad. Tracking data revealed the enormous ground he covered, yes, but also the strategic nature of his positioning. Kanté seemed to have an innate sense for being exactly where the ball was going to be, but this wasn't just intuition—it was a data-backed understanding of opposition patterns. This allowed the French manager, Didier Deschamps, to deploy him in ways that disrupted enemy play, essentially nipping attacks in the bud, so to speak.

These player-specific insights were translated into dynamic strategies. If data showed that French striker Olivier Giroud was particularly effective with headers in the penalty box, you could bet that the team would try to win set pieces in dangerous areas. If forward Antoine Griezmann thrived in free roles, the tactical formation would be adjusted midgame to create spaces for him to exploit. Utilizing data, the strategy was never static—it was a fluid entity, adapting in real time to the flow of the game. And all this was made possible through the intelligent use of player tracking systems.

This benefitted the players and coaches but also spilled into the fan experience as well. Every time Coach Deschamps made a strategic adjustment based on this wealth of data, analysts and commentators, armed with the same tools, were quick to break down the implications for millions watching across the globe. The narrative of the game was no longer confined to the visible actions on the pitch but extended into the world of unseen metrics that nevertheless had palpable impacts. The fans could see the game in 4D—adding the dimension of deep analytical insight to the traditional width, length, and depth of the football field.

The French team's use of player tracking systems in their quest for World Cup glory didn't play a simple supporting role; it was a multi-layered approach that improved performance, deepened strategies, and transformed how fans around the world engaged with the beautiful game—a revolution on the pitch that rippled across fan zones, living rooms, and digital platforms, knitting us all into a more intense, intimate relationship with the sport we adore. The advances made in player tracking technology since the 2014 FIFA World Cup didn't just amplify the performance of athletes like Mbappé and Kanté; it also ignited an uprising of solutions to connect more deeply with fans, transforming the way we experience the beautiful game.

So, how did player tracking systems revolutionize fan engagement?

A critical aspect was live statistics. These once-secret numerical treasures were thrown wide open to the global audience. Companies like Opta became household names for any fan keen on the nuances of the sport. They offered real-time data on everything from ball possession to shot accuracy, from tackle success to player heat maps, all in easy-to-digest formats accessible via mobile apps and websites. Moving beyond rudimentary statistics like ball possession percentages, Opta offered multilayered analytics, such as heat maps and shot accuracy coordinates, accessible in real time through apps and websites. This transformed the metrics and the very experience of watching football. Whether it was dissecting the expected goal value of a semifinal shot by Belgian midfielder Kevin De Bruyne or tracking N'Golo Kanté's tackle success rate, Opta allowed fans to be more than spectators. They became real-time analysts, deepening their emotional and intellectual engagement with the sport. The technology didn't serve to just make fans more knowledgeable; it made them far more invested and passionate, elevating the collective football experience into a blend of culture, technology, and sheer passion.

Even FIFA's own website provided a comprehensive live statistics feature, tracking players' performances in real time and offering more than just rudimentary information. The upshot was that fans could be sitting in New York City, in a bar filled with fellow fans, and have a discussion that was as informed and nuanced as that of professional analysts sitting in a studio half a world away. You could contest the merit of Deschamp's latest tactical switch armed with data, including metrics like expected goal values, a concept popularized by analytics websites such as FiveThirtyEight. FiveThirtyEight, founded by statistician and writer Nate Silver, stands as an emblematic pillar in the burgeoning universe of data journalism. Originally a haven for political data analysis, it expanded its scope to embrace sports, economics, and a host of other subjects. In the context of the 2018 FIFA World Cup, FiveThirtyEight became a sanctuary for fans seeking a more cerebral engagement with the match unfolding in front of them. Using advanced statistical models and methodologies, FiveThirtyEight delves into predictive analytics, dissecting the likely outcomes of matches based on a plethora of metrics. With their data, you could argue or assess the wisdom behind Deschamps' decisions based on more than just emotional fervor or conventional wisdom. Instead, fans could navigate the tactical nuances of Deschamps' strategies by arming themselves with meticulously crunched numbers and analytics. This, in essence, turned casual debates into intellectually engaging dialogues, giving the spectator a toolset that was previously the exclusive domain of analysts and insiders.

But where the technological stride truly showed its colors was in the creation of immersive viewing experiences. The brilliance of VR as an emerging technological frontier found its moment in the sports spotlight during the 2018 FIFA World Cup. Orchestrated through a bold collaboration between Oculus and FOX Sports, this experiment in fan engagement struck at the very core of traditional sports viewership. Fans were no longer bound by the parameters of a television screen but transported into a sumptuously designed, virtual VIP suite with a panoramic overlook of the pitch. The true innovation lay in the freedom it granted the spectator. Imagine the ability to virtually stand beside Olivier Giroud as he executed an athletic leap for a header. You could almost sense the tension, the focus, and the sheer athleticism involved. Or consider the experience of positioning yourself behind the goalie to witness Antoine Griezmann's preparation for a free kick and feeling your heart race as the ball curled tantalizingly toward the goal. These experiences were no longer passive or vicarious; VR technology turned these experiences into personalized, almost tactile engagements. And all of this was made possible without leaving the comfort of your living room. Oculus and FOX Sports enhanced the viewing experience, but just as importantly, they shattered the boundaries separating athletes from fans. By leveraging the capabilities of VR technology, they redefined the notion of "presence" within spectator sports. In this new paradigm, the spectator became more than a witness to the events, they became an active participant, breaking down the metaphorical fourth wall that traditionally distanced fans from the athletes they admired.

AR also made a splash, with apps that allowed fans to superimpose live data over real-time action when viewed through a smartphone or tablet. This melding of the digital and physical worlds added another layer to the narrative, giving fans the power to dissect plays in ways previously reserved for post-game analysis. It arrived not as a novelty but as a transformative force, shifting the spotlight onto the real stars of the show—the fans. For these devotees of the beautiful game, AR technology served as both a magnifying glass and a canvas, offering unprecedented levels of engagement and insight.

The software, like Vizrt's LiveView, democratized punditry. In this new experience, any fan with a smartphone or tablet can overlay real-time data onto the live action playing out on their television screens. Fans watching the game no longer needed to wait for post-game breakdowns to delve into statistics and strategies. A simple swipe of a finger could reveal Kylian Mbappé's acceleration rates, or the odds of a goal being scored from a particular position on the field thanks to the access that LiveView provided. This paradigm shift saw an influx of readily available professional-grade data, empowering fans to transform from spectators into savvy analysts.

Whether debating in living rooms or sharing insights on social media platforms like X (formerly known as Twitter) and Reddit, this informed and engaged fanbase created a new form of collective intelligence around the sport. This fusion of the digital and physical worlds catalyzed a profound alteration in the very anatomy of fandom. It transcended passive watching to impart a complex, layered, and intellectual enjoyment of soccer, rewired the core culture of sports viewership, elevating it into a more interactive and intellectually engaging realm. The 2018 FIFA World Cup emerged as a milestone in the evolution of sports engagement. Fortified by advances in AR, it ruptured conventional molds and forged new standards further energizing an industry that thrives on the fervor of its audience. It stood as a compelling testament to the power of technology in narrowing the divide between on-field action and living-room spectators, forever altering how the world interacts with and relishes the sport it cherishes.

Live-streaming services took it a step further by offering "fan features," such as the ability to overlay player statistics in real time, pause, and even sketch possible plays over the live action. These services were typically part of premium subscription packages, but their growing popularity signaled an appetite for enriched viewing experiences. With live streaming services replete with fan features, the digital world was not merely mimicking the traditional broadcast experience; it was intensifying it, adding layers of interactivity and real-time data analysis that turned fans from mere spectators into active participants in the unfolding drama. For example, streaming services like YouTube TV offered premium features that allowed fans to overlay player statistics in real time, providing an in-depth understanding of each athlete's contribution to the match. More than just numbers, these statistics became fodder for real-time discussions among fans, who now had the ability to validate their intuitions with hard data.

Referencing industry-standard reports such as Nielsen's "State of the Media: Consumer Usage Report," which highlighted the burgeoning trend of sports viewership via streaming platforms, it becomes evident that these value-added fan experiences are far from mere trends or novelties. Instead, they represent a tectonic shift in the landscape of consumer behavior and expectations. According to a report by Conviva, a real-time measurement and intelligence platform for streaming TV, the opening match between Russia and Saudi Arabia alone saw a 742 percent increase in streaming viewership compared to the average of the three previous World Cup opening matches. Conviva's data also showed that the tournament broke the then-record for the most-streamed sporting event, with billions of streaming minutes reported across platforms. Cloud delivery platform Akamai reports that viewers of the first round of the Russia 2018 World Cup streamed 65 percent more data over the Akamai Intelligent Platform than they did during the whole of the Rio World Cup just four years earlier. The number of streams running concurrently hit a record 9.7 million when Mexico played Sweden at the same time as South Korea played Germany on June 27, 2018. The viewing peak the company recorded hit 5 million for the entire tournament in Rio. The highest numbers of streaming came from streaming devices Roku, Chromecast, and PlayStation, which clocked in at 115 minutes each, followed by Xbox at 111 minutes and Apple TV at 107 minutes of viewing time on average per unique viewer.

But the innovations didn't stop there. These platforms allowed fans to pause the action and, using tools akin to those employed by professional sports analysts, sketch out possible plays over the live stream, strategizing in real time. This level of interactivity was more than just a neat feature; it represented a fundamental shift in the fan experience. According to a study by Cisco's Annual Internet Report, the proliferation of these features was directly correlated to increasing broadband speeds and the global adoption of smart devices. In other words, technology served to enhance the viewing experience; it was also actively reshaping the expectations of fans who were hungry to engage at deeper levels.

In the throes of the 2018 FIFA World Cup, this evolution found its proving ground. As France's young stars galvanized their nation's hopes, the technological undercurrents of live streaming services worked to democratize the football intellect, leveling the playing field between the armchair strategist and the paid analyst. It was as if every fan were given a seat in the coach's box, a pencil for sketching plays, and a microphone for live commentary. These fan features, often part of premium subscription packages, moved beyond gimmickry to answer an unspoken yet palpable demand—a hunger for a more intricate, more engaged, more empowered form of sports viewership. This trend was more than evident; it was quantified, examined, and understood to be the new norm in a world where the boundary between the game on the field and the fan in the living room continued to blur. It was here, in the world's most-watched sporting event, that the future of fan engagement was not just predicted but lived, not just imagined but experienced.

In the 2018 FIFA World Cup, the significance of video analysis software as an indispensable ally to teams was on full display, its impact echoing far beyond the tactical headquarters of football squads. For instance, the French national team—ultimately the champions of the tournament— deployed an advanced version of video analytics software, breaking down their own movements and those of their opponents. According to a SportTechie report, coaches could access real-time heat maps, player metrics, and predictive play outcomes, offering them critical tactical advantages.

This technology does far more than tallying stats; it's a platform for intricate analysis that feeds directly into real-time tactical adjustments and long-term strategic plans. Take the match between France and Argentina, where French midfielder N'Golo Kanté was positioned in a way to neutralize Argentina's Lionel Messi's playmaking abilities. The coaching staff made this decision based on hundreds of data points collected and analyzed before and during the match. They dissected Messi's movements, passing channels, and dribbling paths, essentially decoding his style of play to minimize his impact. It was a masterstroke of tactical nuance fueled by rigorous data analysis.

The software's capability to perform granular examinations is game-changing. Teams can scrutinize specific plays, like set pieces or counterattacks, to find weak spots in the opposition or to improve their own execution. This reservoir of data is an invaluable resource for tactical planning as well as for player development. The French team, for example, used these analyses to optimize individual performances, analyzing key factors such as pass accuracy, tackle effectiveness, and shot conversion rates for each player.

Moreover, the significance of video analysis software isn't confined to just coaching staff or players. Advanced platforms are integrating fan experiences into the mix. Several companies rolled out fan-facing applications that allowed viewers to dissect plays, virtually putting them in the coach's seat. This pivotal shift in fan engagement was highlighted during the 2018 FIFA World Cup when companies unveiled platforms geared specifically toward the viewing public, offering a new level of interactivity that goes beyond simply watching the game.

Consider the initiatives of companies like IBM Watson, which used artificial intelligence (AI) to curate highlight reels based on individual fan preferences, essentially crafting a personalized "greatest moments" package for each user. These reels could then be broken down, play by play, allowing fans to understand the tactical nuances and player decisions that contributed to each highlight. These innovations reflect a deeper shift in the fan experience—moving from passive viewership to active engagement. Fans were no longer just spectators but also analysts, strategists, and keen observers who could immerse themselves in the nitty-gritty details of the game. This deepens their understanding and appreciation of the sport but also creates a more communal and interactive experience. Chat forums and social media platforms were abuzz with fans sharing their analyses and insights, contributing to the online dialogue, and fostering a sense of community among fans scattered across the globe. By democratizing access to this kind of analytical depth, video analysis software has effectively bridged the gap between the professional sport and its fan base. It's not merely a tool for in-game strategy and opponent analysis anymore; it's a conduit for richer, more nuanced fan engagement, adding a new layer to the narrative of the game.

As the first World Cup to implement VAR, the 2018 tournament became a very public case study for exploring the benefits and challenges that this technology brings to the game of football. The technology itself is a complex combination of high-definition cameras positioned around the stadium, which capture multiple angles of gameplay. These feeds are then monitored in real time by a team of assistant referees stationed in a VAR control room. When a contentious moment occurs—be it a potential penalty, offside, or mistaken identity—the on-field referee can pause the game and consult with the VAR team. In some instances, the referee reviews the footage on a monitor on the side of the pitch. This system aims to make the sport fairer, helping referees avoid critical errors that could otherwise go undetected. In terms of its impact on the 2018 tournament, VAR unquestionably had a polarizing effect. According to FIFA, VAR reviewed 335 incidents across 64 matches, an average of 5.2 checks per game. Out of those reviews, 14 led to a change in referee decisions. However, it was the nature and magnitude of these reversed decisions that led to debates, uproars, and in some cases, cheers. Decisions that were upheld or reversed included granting penalties that were initially missed to rescinding red cards, and VAR had a hand in shaping the narratives of multiple matches. One example is Portugal's game against Iran. Cristiano Ronaldo was awarded a penalty after a VAR review, a moment that kept Portugal's hopes alive in that game. But Ronaldo himself later became the subject of a VAR review for an off-the-ball incident, although he ended up receiving just a yellow card.

The pivotal moment, however, came during the final between France and Croatia. As described earlier, a VAR decision led to a penalty that changed the course of the game. While it amplified the voice of skeptics who argue that VAR disrupts the flow of the game and introduces its own form of error, it also showed that VAR could work in high-stakes scenarios to correct what might be considered "obvious" mistakes. The challenge, then, is to define what constitutes a "clear and obvious error." Critics argue that the technology undermines the authority of on-field referees and opens a Pandora's box of interpretive debates that could detract from the game's natural flow. Fans have also expressed concern over how VAR breaks can deflate the energetic atmosphere of a match, especially when those in the stadium are left in the dark about what's being reviewed.

Yet, for every criticism, there's a counterpoint emphasizing VAR's ability to bring justice to a sport that has long been marred by human error. Proponents say that while VAR may not be perfect, it adds an invaluable layer of scrutiny that could lead to fairer outcomes. Moreover, the fan engagement in these tournaments has also been influenced positively in many ways by VAR. The suspense, the debates, and even the memes that follow a VAR decision have become a part of the modern football experience.

VAR's debut in the 2018 World Cup acted as both a case study and a catalyst for what the future of football might look like. While it illuminated the challenges that come with integrating technology into a deeply traditional sport, it also set the stage for ongoing refinements in how VAR is implemented. In the quest for a perfectly officiated game, VAR seems here to stay, its influence likely to grow and evolve in subsequent tournaments.

For as much as the 2018 FIFA World Cup was a spectacle of human endeavor and skill, it was equally a landmark event in fan engagement, leveraging player tracking systems, video analysis software, and complementary technologies to create more informed, enriched, and immersive experiences. Fans were no longer passive recipients of the action but active participants in the narrative, armed with insights and offered vantage points that brought them closer than ever to the sport they love.

In the era of unprecedented data-driven transformation, the ethical dimensions cannot be ignored. It is crucial to recognize that governing bodies and organizations have put certain mechanisms in place to mitigate privacy and ethical concerns, particularly during the 2018 FIFA World Cup. Firstly, FIFA's own Data Protection Policy has been designed to ensure the highest level of security for all types of data collected during the tournament. According to FIFA's official policy, the organization adheres to strict guidelines regarding data collection, usage, and protection in compliance with the General Data Protection Regulation (GDPR) of the European Union. This legal framework has set new precedents in ensuring that data privacy and ethical considerations are respected but have the potential to be institutionalized.

FIFA partnered with cybersecurity companies to protect the integrity of the digital fan experience. Cisco, for instance, provided advanced firewall and malware protection for the 2018 event, aiming to secure data in transit and at rest. This partnership offered an additional layer of protection that sought to protect the data integrity of both players and fans alike. Additionally, the apps and platforms that provide enriched fan experiences also often have robust privacy policies. Companies like Opta, with its real-time statistics and streaming services like FOX Sports have data protection measures that are designed to comply with international data protection regulations. These measures include encryption, two-factor authentication (2FA), and stringent data access policies.

However, no system can be completely infallible. Cybersecurity companies recorded an increase in phishing attacks and cybersecurity threats around the time of the World Cup, attempting to exploit the public's heightened interest in the event. This illustrates the ongoing battle between advancing technology and the preservation of ethical integrity. Therefore, as we live through this seismic technological shift that's upending our very understanding of sports fandom, it's imperative to take a balanced view. Technologies that bring unprecedented convenience and connection also bring challenges to our ethical standards and privacy norms. Yet, with robust policies and vigilant cybersecurity measures in place, the 2018 FIFA World Cup served as a lesson that the path to technological progress doesn't have to trample upon ethical landscapes.

In a world shrunk by technology, the 2018 FIFA World Cup was more than a football tournament being played in Russia. It was a microcosm of global inclusivity and accessibility, channeled through the veins of digital conduits. Advancements in inclusivity and fan engagement included breaking down age-old linguistic barriers that would otherwise isolate large swaths of fans. The old way of broadcasting in a single language, based on the location of the game being played or the talent in the broadcast booth, was relegated to the past, as FIFA's digital platforms became the epitome of global citizenship, offering content in a multitude of languages to cater to a truly international audience. This was more than a simple gesture of goodwill; it translated into real engagement. Websites and mobile apps dynamically adapted to users' language preferences, dissolving linguistic barriers that might have previously alienated non-English-speaking fans. According to a report from FluentU, multilingual platforms can increase user engagement by up to 40 percent. In fact, FIFA reported that their multilingual digital platforms drew a record-breaking 7.5 billion engagements during the 2018 World Cup, an unprecedented number that attests to the efficacy of their global outreach strategies.

Recognizing that the digital sphere must be as accessible as the physical one, FIFA forged partnerships with tech firms such as AudioEye to ensure their platforms met the rigorous Web Content Accessibility Guidelines (WCAG). This decision was more than a token compliance gesture; it represented a genuine commitment to creating a more inclusive fan experience. From offering screen reader compatibility to integrating closed captioning, FIFA used technology to expand accessibility features, allowing fans with disabilities to engage with the sport in a more meaningful way. In fact, according to the FIFA Digital Report 2018, these enhancements contributed to a surge in engagement across all demographics, emphasizing that when you broaden the net of accessibility, the entire sporting community benefits.

In the 2018 World Cup, FIFA took exemplary steps in making the event accessible to fans with disabilities, partnering with companies like AudioEye to meet the stringent WCAG. This initiative was not a "tick the box" exercise; it was about broadening the scope of who could fully engage with the sport. FIFA's digital platforms were designed to be compatible with screen readers and featured closed captioning. According to the FIFA Digital Report 2018, these enhancements ensured compliance with accessibility guidelines but also led to a tangible increase in fan engagement across all demographics, proving that inclusivity and technology can join forces to make the sport universally cherished.

The social media phenomenon had already been deeply ingrained into daily life by the time the 2018 FIFA World Cup came around. The social networks wove intricate patterns between people that transcended borders and time zones. The integration of platforms like Twitter, Instagram, and Facebook served as the twine, fostering an interconnected and buzzing global community. Fans were no longer confined to the 90 minutes of gameplay or to localized banter. Twitter's live event pages, for instance, acted like virtual stadiums, complete with real-time polls and ongoing commentary. Fans became not just spectators but active participants in the World Cup narrative. According to Twitter data, the hashtag #WorldCup2018 exploded with more than 10 million mentions, a testament to the electric charge social engagement sent through the global fan community. The sheer volume of mentions was more than just a statistical high point; it was a cultural and emotional lightning rod, illuminating the profound role social media has come to play in modern sports fandom. Each tweet, retweet, or mention wasn't merely an interaction; it was an electrifying connection, linking fans across continents, languages, and loyalties. Whether it was dissecting a controversial referee decision, celebrating a last-minute goal, or sharing collective agony over a missed penalty, these mentions created a web of emotional high-fidelity that made the World Cup a universal experience, becoming so much more than a televised sporting event.

This eruption of social engagement also had a ripple effect, impacting everything from real-time analytics for advertisers to strategies for content creators who hopped onto the bandwagon, churning out videos, memes, and articles that further stoked the fan fervor. It turned the global conversation into a self-sustaining ecosystem, fueled by the raw energy of millions of fans. And in that virtual world, people found unity; the hashtag became a universal rallying cry, a meeting place for debate, and a stage for the expression of pure emotion.

Yet, it wasn't about superficial interaction; it was also about depth and meaning. Through partnerships with tech companies like Google and Alibaba, FIFA ventured beyond the standard social media offerings into the realm of gamification. Take the FIFA World Cup Fantasy game, for instance. Fans could create their dream teams, amass points based on real-world player performances, and compete against friends and strangers alike, all while climbing global leaderboards. This was no mere pastime; it was a fully immersive experience that tapped into the competitive spirit that fuels sports fandom.

Virtual rewards, from exclusive digital stickers to unlockable videos, made each game and each goal a doubly rewarding experience, both in the real world and in the digital universe. This addition of gamified elements appealed to another layer of fan psychology, morphing passive spectators into active participants. Suddenly, you were more than just a fan; you were a competitor, a pundit, a vital part of a massive digital ecosystem that fed off every pass, every goal, every heart-stopping save.

And let's not forget social ranking systems, a sort of digital pecking order that, far from creating division, fostered a sense of community and pride. Fans were naturally bound by the love for their team or the thrill of the game, but they were united in a complex yet enriching digital hierarchy that turned every match into a multilevel experience of shared aspirations, victories, and defeats.

According to the GlobalWebIndex, 53 percent of 16- to 64-year-olds said they played an online game via a smartphone in the last month, showing the proclivity of the audience for gamified experiences. FIFA capitalized on this by turning what could have been a mere sporting spectacle into an interactive, multifaceted global event unlike any other. The merging of social media and gamified experiences transcended the traditional boundaries of fandom, creating an international confluence of culture, competition, and camaraderie. As fans navigated this intricate maze of technology and emotion, the 2018 World Cup evolved from a mere sporting event into a global cultural phenomenon, affirming that the future of fan engagement is a rich tapestry woven from countless digital threads.

In essence, technology's role in the 2018 Cup redefined how the game is played and how the game is experienced. The marriage of technology and sports during the 2018 FIFA World Cup rewrote the script, rewriting the way football is executed on the pitch, but going deeper and rewriting how it's relished in living rooms and pubs around the world, making it a multidimensional feast of sight, sound, and real-time statistics. It served as a microcosm of what is achievable when technology, collaboration, and fan-centric planning converge. It didn't just set a new standard for sporting events, it showcased a model for leveraging technology to make global events more inclusive, more interactive, and infinitely more engaging. In a synergistic blend of athletic prowess, technological innovation, and fan-centric planning, the French victory epitomized the future of sports in an increasingly digital world, capturing the essence of what makes the World Cup a truly global phenomenon.

Welcome to football in the digital age—in this age, it is far more than a game; it's an experience, an experience that culminated in the thrilling Cup final that saw France overcome Croatia's spirited challenge at Moscow's Luzhniki Stadium by a score of 4-2. Didier Deschamps led his French team to a World Cup win that had as much to do with on-field brilliance as it did with behind-the-scenes technological finesse. Despite Croatia's gallant performance and the ensuing debates around VAR decisions, France emerged victorious, boasting a well-rounded team replete with talent like Antoine Griezmann and Kylian Mbappé. The game, a blend of excitement, controversy, and finesse, was a fan-engaging spectacle with one of the highest goal tallies in a final since 1958.

Behind the French victory, however, was the power of technology. Employing advanced video analysis software, the French team undertook meticulous planning and strategy refinement that proved crucial in their triumph. This was part of a broader digital landscape surrounding the 2018 FIFA World Cup, featuring partnerships with tech giants like IBM for analytics and Cisco for cybersecurity. The data-driven tactics paid off. This is particularly evident in how France navigated through complex defensive setups. The synergy between human talent and technological insight was epitomized in the second-half goals from Paul Pogba and Kylian Mbappé against Croatia. The positions they took up, the timing of their runs, and even the exact areas where they aimed their shots could be traced back to insights derived from video analysis. But it wasn't just the outfield players. Even Hugo Lloris, the goalkeeper, benefitted from tech-driven analysis, which helped him anticipate the play patterns and shot directions of opposing strikers, despite the hiccup that led to Croatia's second goal in the finals. The reach of technology went beyond just enhancing the athletes' performance; it also enriched the viewer's experience. Advanced platforms like IBM Watson provided fans with tools to dissect plays, turning them into virtual coaches, and Twitter came alive with more than 10 million mentions, signifying the global engagement the technology facilitated.

France's victory symbolized more than just athletic prowess. Their victory epitomized the pinnacle of what modern technology can add to sport, elevating the event from a local game to a global, immersive, and highly interactive spectacle.

Digital Activism

2019 Women's World Cup: United States Victory

In the scorching summer of 2019, France became the epicenter of the soccer universe, hosting the eighth edition of the FIFA Women's World Cup. The air was thick with anticipation. The streets of cities like Paris, Lyon, and Nice were buzzing with excitement. The flags of the participating nations hung from balconies, and the chatter of multiple languages filled the air, a testament to the global pull of the event. Soccer fans from around the world descended upon the French cities, their faces painted in national colors, spirits high, and voices ready to cheer. Stadiums were transformed into communities of emotion, where every goal was met with roars that seemed to shake the very foundations of the venues. The atmosphere was electric, a heady mix of competition, national pride, and the sheer joy that comes from being part of something larger than oneself. For those few weeks, soccer was more than a game; it was a unifying force that transcended borders, languages, and cultures. Millions of fans tuned in from every corner of the globe, their eyes glued to screens big and small, all captivated by the drama unfolding on the French turf.

Amidst this backdrop, the U.S. Women's National Team (USWNT) arrived, not just as defending champions but as crusaders for a cause that extended beyond the white lines of the soccer field. They were a powerhouse, yes, but they were also pioneers in a fight that had long been simmering: gender equity. The team, led by co-captains Megan Rapinoe and Alex Morgan was acutely aware that their platform was bigger than sports; it was a stage from which they could challenge societal norms and ignite conversations that mattered. Their campaign was a dual mission, a two-front war fought on grass and screens. On the field, they displayed extraordinary skill, teamwork, and determination. Off the field, they were equally formidable, leveraging the power of social media to take their message to the masses. Hashtags and posts calling for gender equity became their digital rallying cries, as potent as any goal or assist in amplifying their message. Instagram posts offered glimpses into their lives and struggles, humanizing them and, by extension, the cause they represented.

In an era where smartphones have become extensions of our hands and social media platforms have become the new town squares, the digital realm has emerged as a potent force for change. The USWNT, astute and forward-thinking, recognized this transformative shift early on. They saw a world where boundaries were dissolving, where a tweet sent from a locker room in Lyon could resonate in a living room in Los Angeles or a café in Lagos within seconds.

The speed of digital communication became a metaphorical advantage for the team. Just as a soccer ball, when kicked with precision, can swiftly find its way into the net, a well-crafted tweet or post could instantly capture the attention of millions. The USWNT understood that, in this digital age, their voices, amplified by technology, had the velocity to outpace traditional means of communication. A single tweet, imbued with emotion and purpose, could travel faster than any soccer ball, crossing continents and oceans in the blink of an eye.

The vastness of the digital audience was unparalleled. Stadiums, no matter how colossal, have a limit to the number of spectators they can accommodate, but the digital arena knows no such bounds. An Instagram post, capturing a candid moment of camaraderie or a poignant plea for equality, had the potential to reach an audience that dwarfed the capacity of any physical venue. The USWNT's digital footprint extended far beyond the confines of the stadiums they played in, touching hearts and minds across the globe. But perhaps the most powerful tool in their digital arsenal was the hashtag. In the hands of the USWNT, hashtags became more than just digital tags; they transformed into rallying cries, symbols of a movement. These concise, potent phrases encapsulated the essence of their fight. They were banners under which supporters, regardless of their geographical location, could unite. Whether it was

#EqualPay or #DareToShine, the hashtags became digital beacons, drawing in supporters from all walks of life. They created virtual marches, where millions, armed with keyboards and touchscreens, marched side-by-side in solidarity with the team's cause.

#EqualPay was a hashtag that became a rallying cry. The origins of #EqualPay can be traced back to a long-standing issue that was not unique to the world of sports: the gender pay gap. Women across various professions have long been advocating for equal pay for equal work. However, when the USWNT took up this mantle, they brought with them the spotlight of the global stage. The hashtag was not born overnight. It was the culmination of years of frustration and advocacy. The team's fight for equal pay was initiated long before the World Cup, with players voicing their concerns about the stark wage disparities between the men's and women's teams. But it was in the lead-up to the 2019 tournament that #EqualPay gained significant traction, becoming synonymous with the team's dual mission: to win the Cup and to fight for gender equity.

Megan Rapinoe, with her distinctive purple hair and unwavering conviction, became the face of this movement. Her iconic stance, arms outstretched in a defiant celebration after scoring a goal, was not just a moment of athletic triumph; it was a statement. That image, paired with the hashtag #EqualPay, went viral, encapsulating the team's resolve and the broader message of gender equity. Rapinoe's celebration became a symbol of defiance against systemic inequalities, resonating with millions worldwide.

Whereas #EqualPay was a grassroots movement from the team and its supporters, #DareToShine was initially introduced by FIFA, the governing body of world soccer, as the official slogan for the 2019 Women's World Cup. Intended to highlight the brilliance of the female athletes and the spirit of the game, the U.S. team saw an opportunity to coopt this message for their own advocacy. They dared to shine, not just on the field, but in challenging the status quo. By aligning their fight for equal pay with FIFA's own promotional hashtag, the USWNT cleverly intertwined their message with the broader narrative of the tournament, ensuring that discussions about their performance were inseparable from discussions about gender equity.

In harnessing the power of digital activism, the USWNT did more than just communicate; they galvanized. They turned passive observers into active participants, creating a global community united by a shared vision of equality and justice. Through tweets, posts, and hashtags, they crafted a narrative that was not only compelling but also contagious, spreading like wildfire in the vast expanse of the digital world. So, as the tournament unfolded, it became crystal clear that this Women's World Cup was a great deal more than the exciting soccer games being played throughout France. It was about using the global stage to spotlight issues that had long been sidelined. It was about sports and technology coming together in a powerful alliance to advocate for change. And above all, it was about a group of extraordinary athletes who realized that they had the power to change the world, both on and off the field.

The growing digital-first age in 2019 offered a unique advantage. That was the ability to measure impact. Analytics revealed the staggering reach of these hashtags. #EqualPay was mentioned millions of times across various social media platforms during the tournament, with spikes in activity correlating with key moments, such as Rapinoe's iconic goals. Similarly, #DareToShine saw a surge in usage, especially when paired with discussions about equal pay. These numbers, however, tell only part of the story. Beyond the metrics, the real impact lay in the global conversations these hashtags ignited. They rose above the soccer pitch and started to spark debates in boardrooms, classrooms, and living rooms around the world. The hashtags became rallying cries, uniting people across different backgrounds in a shared quest for equality.

In the end, the hashtag revolution of the 2019 Women's World Cup was a testament to the power of digital activism. Through concise, potent messages, the USWNT managed to turn a soccer tournament into a global movement for change. In the digital age, athletes are no longer just competitors on the field; they are influencers, advocates, and change-makers in the online realm. With the power of social media at their fingertips, players can reach millions, shaping narratives and driving conversations. Two players, Megan Rapinoe, who became the face of the #EqualPay hashtag movement, and Alex Morgan, the USWNT co-captain, known for her grace on the field and charm off it, stood out during the 2019 Women's World Cup, not just for their on-field brilliance, but for their impactful digital presence. While Rapinoe dominated Twitter, Alex Morgan's realm was Instagram. She had amassed a significant following on the platform, making her one of the most influential figures in women's sports.

Morgan's Instagram posts were not just about glamorous photos or brand endorsements. During the 2019 World Cup, they became a window into the lives of the players, offering fans a behind-the-scenes look at their journey. From candid locker-room moments to training sessions, from personal reflections to group celebrations, Morgan's posts humanized the team, making their struggle for equality relatable and real. One of the most impactful aspects of her Instagram presence was the way she showcased the camaraderie and sisterhood within the team. Through stories and posts, fans got a glimpse of the bonds that held the USWNT together, making their fight for equal pay not just a legal battle, but a deeply personal one. By sharing these intimate moments, Morgan underscored the idea that, behind every hashtag, every protest, and every goal, there were real women with real stories, all united in a shared mission.

In essence, while the digital field was different from the grassy pitches of France, the goal remained the same for players like Rapinoe and Morgan: to make a difference. Through their respective platforms, they showcased the power of digital activism, proving that in the modern age, the game is played both on and off the field.

Every movement, no matter how powerful its message, needs amplifiers. These are voices or influencers who can take the core message and broadcast it to a wider audience, magnifying its impact. For the USWNT's digital activism campaign during the 2019 Women's World Cup, these amplifiers came in various forms, from celebrities and influencers to traditional media and passionate fans.

The support of high-profile celebrities and influencers played a pivotal role in propelling the USWNT's message into the global spotlight. Tennis legend Serena Williams, a trailblazer in her own right, voiced her support for the team's fight for equal pay, drawing parallels to her own battles in the tennis world. Her endorsement, given her stature in the sports world, added significant weight to the cause. Talk show host Ellen DeGeneres, together with her massive following, also championed the team's cause. Through tweets, show segments, and interviews, Ellen not only celebrated the team's on-field achievements but also highlighted their off-field advocacy, bringing the conversation about gender equity in sports to her vast audience.

The backing of such influential figures amplified the team's message exponentially. Their endorsements served as a testament to the universality of the USWNT's fight, showing that the quest for gender equity resonated beyond the confines of soccer. These voices added fuel to the fire around equality that the USWNT started at the 2019 World Cup.

Social media was the primary battleground for the USWNT's digital activism, but traditional media outlets played a crucial role in giving their campaign a mainstream platform. Outlets like ESPN and the *New York Times* provided extensive coverage of the team's dual mission, weaving narratives that combined athletic prowess with social advocacy. Developing features, op-eds, and in-depth analyses in these outlets contextualized the team's fight, tracing the history of gender disparities in sports and highlighting the broader implications of the USWNT's campaign. By doing so, these traditional and highly respected channels bridged the gap between the digital realm and traditional media consumers. This helped ensure that their message reached every corner of society.

The digital age has democratized content creation, allowing fans to become active participants in shaping narratives. For the USWNT, fan-generated content became a powerful tool in spreading their message. Memes, fan art, GIFs, and videos created by supporters flooded social media platforms, each piece of content serving as a testament to the grassroots support the team enjoyed. This content, often humorous but always poignant, added a layer of relatability to the team's campaign. It showcased the creativity and passion of the fans, turning them from passive spectators into advocates for the cause.

One of the most iconic moments of the 2019 Women's World Cup was Alex Morgan's "tea-sipping" celebration after scoring against England. This gesture, a playful nod to the Boston Tea Party, quickly became a viral sensation, with fans and even celebrities emulating the pose. Beyond the humor, the "tea-sipping" meme became a symbol of defiance and empowerment. It was coopted by fans and used as a rallying cry for the team's fight for equal pay. The meme's widespread adoption and adaptation showcased the power of digital content in driving narratives, turning a simple goal celebration into a statement of purpose.

These amplifiers, whether they were celebrities, media outlets, or fans, all played a crucial role in the success of the USWNT's digital activism campaign. They took the team's message and broadcast it far and wide, ensuring that the call for gender equity echoed in every corner of the globe.

The role social media played in widespread access to instant messaging and the power of real-time communications was on full display during the 2019 World Cup. It offers immediacy and a direct connection between the source and the audience, allowing for a dynamic exchange of ideas and emotions. For the USWNT, real-time digital platforms became instrumental in their activism, providing them with tools to engage, inform, and rally their supporters as events unfolded. While the matches were broadcast globally, a parallel narrative was crafted on platforms like Twitter. Live tweeting became more than just a play-by-play commentary; it was a platform for advocacy. Every goal, foul, and controversial decision not just described but contextualized within the larger framework of the team's fight for equality.

In the pulsating world of live sports, where every second counts and emotions run high, the real-time commentary offered by the USWNT added a layer of depth and context that was both enlightening and impactful. Fans, glued to their screens, were treated to more than just a display of exceptional soccer skills; they were given a window into the very soul of the team, their aspirations, and the hurdles they continually overcame. This dual narrative, seamlessly woven into the fabric of each match, painted a vivid picture. On the one hand, there was the undeniable athletic brilliance of the team. Each pass, goal, and defensive maneuver is a testament to their dedication, training, and talent. On the other, there was the stark reality of the systemic challenges they grappled with—challenges that extended far beyond the confines of the soccer field and delved deep into societal norms and biases.

Every match became more than just a quest for victory; it was a story of resilience, of a group of women who, even in the face of adversity, showcased skill, determination, and an unwavering spirit of defiance. The live tweets, punctuated by the now-iconic hashtags, were not merely updates on the game's progress. They were powerful statements, echoing the team's dual mission. Each tweet, each hashtag, served as a clarion call, reminding fans and spectators of the larger battle for equality that raged alongside the on-field action.

The genius of this approach lay in its ability to intertwine two narratives—sporting excellence and the quest for gender equity—into a singular, compelling storyline. It ensured that while fans reveled in the adrenaline rush of the game, they were also constantly reminded of the broader context, the deeper significance of each match. The thrill of a goal or a deft maneuver was amplified by the knowledge of what it represented: a step forward, not just in the tournament, but in the ongoing journey toward a more just and equitable world.

Beyond the matches, the players utilized platforms like Instagram Live to connect directly with their fans. These sessions, often candid and unscripted, provided a rare glimpse into the minds of the athletes. Co-captains Megan Rapinoe and Alex Morgan took to the platform to answer questions, address concerns, and share their personal experiences. These Q&A sessions tackled the hard questions: the challenges of advocating for change while representing one's country, the backlash they faced, and the personal toll of their advocacy. By addressing these issues head-on, in real time, the players humanized their struggle, making it relatable to millions of fans worldwide. It showcased their vulnerability, determination, and unwavering commitment to the cause, further endearing them to their supporters.

In an era where every click, like, and share leaves a digital footprint, data has ascended to the throne as the reigning monarch of influence. It's the silent observer, capturing the nuances of online interactions and painting a vivid picture of the digital landscape. The USWNT, strategically ahead of the curve, keenly understood the transformative power of data. Harnessing the capabilities of real-time analytics, they embarked on a journey to meticulously craft their narrative. Every post they shared, every tweet they dispatched, and every live session they conducted was not just a message in the vast digital ocean but a beacon, sending out signals and awaiting responses. By keeping a vigilant eye on metrics such as reach, engagement, and the often-intangible sentiment, they were able to tap directly into the heartbeats and emotions of their vast audience.

This wasn't just about counting likes or retweets; it was a deeper dive into understanding the very tenor of their audience's reactions. Were their messages resonating? Were they sparking joy, anger, or debate? Were they igniting the fires of change or merely simmering in the background? These were the questions that real-time analytics sought to answer. Armed with this treasure trove of insights, the USWNT could deftly pivot their strategies. If a particular message was soaring and capturing imaginations, they could amplify it. If another was missing the mark or generating misconceptions, they could recalibrate and clarify. This dynamic approach, rooted in data, allowed them to be both reactive and proactive, ensuring that their digital activism was not just a shout into the void but a resonant chorus in a very carefully constructed and well-orchestrated grand symphony.

The USWNT's efficient and carefully managed use of real-time analytics was a master class in digital strategy. It showcased their commitment not only to speaking but also to listening, adapting, and evolving in tandem with their audience, ensuring that their crusade for equality was as impactful online as it was on the pitch. This data-driven approach allowed the team to delve deep into the heartbeats and emotions of their supporters. They could discern the stories that truly struck a chord, the messages that ignited passion, and the areas that perhaps needed a renewed focus or a different approach. It provided them with insights into the global conversations around their campaign, enabling them to tailor their digital activism for maximum impact. Armed with this knowledge, the USWNT was able to fine-tune their digital activism, ensuring that every tweet, post, and live session was calibrated for maximum resonance and impact.

The USWNT's audacious blend of athletic prowess and digital advocacy set a precedent for teams and athletes worldwide. Their message, amplified by the power of social media, resonated with players in different sports and regions, all of whom faced their own battles against inequality and prejudice. From female cricketers in South Asia to rugby players in

Africa, the USWNT's campaign became a beacon of hope and a blue-print for change, rooted in the pursuit of equality and justice. It not only captured the imaginations of millions but also inspired change on a global scale. Teams from all around the world began to harness the power of social media to share their stories, highlight disparities, and rally support. The narrative shifted from a mere celebration of athletic achievements to a broader conversation on rights, representation, and respect. The USWNT's digital activism had effectively sown the seeds for a global movement.

The impact of the USWNT's campaign was not limited to the digital realm. Their persistent advocacy, bolstered by the global support they garnered, began to influence the very policies and structures that governed the sport. The U.S. Soccer Federation, long criticized for its perceived gender biases, found itself at the epicenter of a global debate on pay equity. The pressure mounted, leading to increased scrutiny, discussions, and eventually, policy revisions.

On a larger scale, FIFA could not remain impervious to the tidal wave of change. The conversations around equal pay, fair representation, and gender equity began to feature prominently in its agendas. While the road to comprehensive reform was long, the wheels had been set in motion, all thanks to the digital echoes of the USWNT's campaign.

In the Southern Hemisphere, amidst the vast landscapes of Australia, a remarkable chapter in the annals of sports equality was being written. The global movement for gender equity in sports, catalyzed by the USWNT's fervent campaign, found resonance in the heart of the Australian continent. The Australian women's soccer team, affectionately christened the Matildas, became the torchbearers of this movement Down Under.

Drawing inspiration from the USWNT's digital activism and fortified with compelling data and poignant narratives of their own, the Matildas embarked on a formidable challenge against their national federation. This wasn't just a skirmish over contracts; it was a profound statement against years of systemic disparities and ingrained biases. As the Matildas' campaign gained momentum, both on the verdant soccer pitches and in the digital realm, it captured the imagination of the Australian populace. Tales of their arduous journeys, the challenges they faced, and the sheer determination with which they overcame obstacles stood in stark contrast to their awe-inspiring achievements on the global stage. These narratives, deeply human and relatable, transformed into a clarion call for change that reverberated across the nation.

The Australian media, often known for its fierce independence, amplified these stories, bringing them to the forefront of national discourse.

Corporate sponsors, recognizing the shifting tides and the moral imperative of the cause, lent their weight to the Matildas' quest. The collective voice of the nation, from its bustling cities to its serene outback, echoed a singular demand: justice, equality, and respect for the Matildas. The crescendo of this nationwide movement reached its zenith in late 2019. In a moment that would be etched in history, the Matildas achieved a groundbreaking pay deal. This wasn't just about numbers on a contract; it symbolized parity, recognition, and respect. The Matildas were now on an equal footing, in terms of pay and conditions, with their male counterparts.

This monumental agreement, celebrated across the globe, was more than just a victory for the Matildas. It was a triumph for gender equity in sports, a beacon for other teams and athletes worldwide. Above all, it underscored the undeniable might of collective resolve, the potency of well-directed digital advocacy, and the timeless truth that when united, people can usher in transformative change.

As the floodlights were powered off across France's soccer fields and the digital echoes of the USWNT's campaign began to fade, the real battle was only just beginning. The team's advocacy for gender equity, amplified by their World Cup victory and digital activism, had set the stage for a series of consequential events that would shape the future of women's sports in the United States and beyond. The USWNT's impassioned crusade for equal pay and fair conditions did not remain confined to the soccer fields or the digital platforms where their advocacy first took root. Instead, their relentless pursuit of justice propelled the issue from the sports pages to the forefront of national discourse, ultimately echoing in the chambers of the U.S. Congress. The team's vocal demands, coupled with a groundswell of public support, prompted the nation's lawmakers to take notice and act. As a result, a series of congressional hearings were initiated, aiming to probe the depths of the disparities that the USWNT and their counterparts in other sports faced. These hearings were emotionally charged and highly watched, and the raw realities of gender discrimination in sports were laid bare for all to see. Each session was marked by compelling testimonies that ranged from heart-wrenching personal accounts to incisive legal arguments. The atmosphere was often palpable with tension, as witnesses recounted their experiences, challenging the systemic prejudices and deep-seated structural barriers that have historically marginalized women's sports.

A diverse array of voices took to the stand during these hearings. Legal luminaries dissected the nuances of contracts and labor laws, while former players painted vivid pictures of their struggles, contrasting their world-class achievements with the inequities they faced off the field. Representatives from U.S. Soccer, the sport's governing body, were called upon to defend and explain their policies, often facing tough questions and pointed critiques. Notably, members of the USWNT themselves stepped forward, sharing their stories with a mix of grace, determination, and undeniable passion. Their testimonies, enriched by data and personal experiences provided a firsthand account of the challenges they faced, both as world champion athletes and as women in a male-dominated landscape.

As these hearings unfolded, the nation tuned in, collectively holding its breath. Every revelation, every argument, and every piece of evidence was scrutinized, debated, and discussed in homes, offices, and public spaces across the country. But beyond the specifics of pay scales, endorsements, and revenue allocations, these hearings symbolized something far greater. They became a mirror, reflecting a society at a crossroads, wrestling with fundamental questions about gender equity, the value of representation, and the very essence of justice in the modern age. The results of the congressional hearings and the ensuing legal confrontations were felt far and wide, marking pivotal moments in the USWNT's relentless quest for justice. These events, while monumental, were just moments in an ongoing saga. The legal skirmishes did yield results, with U.S. Soccer being nudged into revisiting and revising certain contractual terms and remuneration frameworks. However, the specter of inequality continues to loom large, casting its shadow not only over the realm of soccer but also over a myriad of other sports.

The 2019 campaign of the USWNT, with its blend of on-field brilliance and off-field advocacy, has left a history-defining mark on the world of sports. Its impact is being felt across the globe. For budding female athletes watching from the sidelines, the team's audacity and resilience have become a source of inspiration. They now harbor dreams not just of scoring goals or winning medals, but of shattering glass ceilings and challenging age-old norms. The USWNT's journey has sown in them the seeds of belief, a conviction that they, too, are worthy and capable of honor, recognition, and parity.

Conversely, the campaign has also cast a glaring spotlight on the deep-rooted biases that continue to permeate the sports industry. It serves as a stark reminder that the path to genuine equality is neither straight nor smooth. It is a winding trail, strewn with obstacles and demanding perseverance, tenacity, and an unwavering commitment to the cause. However, in the center of these challenges, one thing is undeniable: the narrative around gender equity in sports has undergone a seismic shift, thanks in no small part to the USWNT's endeavors. What was once whispered in hushed tones or relegated to the fringes of sports discourse is now being discussed openly, debated passionately, and acted upon. Sports teams, leagues, and governing bodies across the globe are being compelled to introspect, to question their entrenched practices, and to chart a more equitable course for the future.

In today's digital age, where information travels at the speed of light and boundaries are rendered almost obsolete, the USWNT's activism has left an indelible mark on the global consciousness. Their digital endeavors, from tweets to posts to live sessions, have traversed continents, breaking barriers of language and culture, reaching even the most remote corners of our planet. These digital echoes have not just been heard; they have sparked debates, fueled grassroots movements, and compelled societies to confront long-standing biases and prejudices.

The ripple effects of their digital activism are as vast as they are varied. From urban centers to rural hamlets, people are discussing, debating, and demanding change, inspired by the USWNT's unwavering commitment to gender equity. The full magnitude of their influence is still revealing itself, but an undeniable sentiment is gaining momentum: a wind of change, driven by the team's passion, determination, and adept use of digital platforms, is sweeping across the globe. This change promises a future where gender equity in sports isn't the exception but the norm.

Reflecting upon that electrifying summer in France, the magnitude of what transpired becomes even more evident. It wasn't just a sporting event; it was a watershed moment in the history of sports and activism. The confluence of athletic excellence with the power of digital advocacy showcased a potent force, one capable of instigating profound societal change. The USWNT, with their victories and challenges, emerged not just as soccer champions but as trailblazers, lighting the path for countless others.

Their journey, marked by highs and lows, triumphs, and trials, stands as a testament to the transformative power of collective action. It serves as a poignant reminder of the potential that lies within each of us. When we find our voices, come together with a shared vision, and leverage the vast digital tools at our fingertips, we possess the power to rewrite narratives, challenge entrenched norms, and shape a future that's brighter, fairer, and more just for all.

Ensuring the Health and Safety of Athletes and Staff

Tokyo 2020 Olympics: COVID-19 Delays

The Olympic flame has always been a symbol of hope, unity, and the collective spirit of humanity. Every four years, this flame lights up the global stage, inviting nations from all over the world to join in a celebration of athleticism and mutual respect. Tokyo, having previously hosted the Olympics in 1964, was gearing up to welcome the world to its shores once again in 2020. The city aimed to showcase its technological advancements while highlighting the rich cultural heritage that Japan is known for. As preparations were underway and athletes around the world were training diligently, the excitement and anticipation for the upcoming Games were growing. However, as the event's date approached, it became evident that the Tokyo 2020 Olympics would face unanticipated challenges. A new health concern, a novel coronavirus, or COVID-19, began to spread globally. This virus, which started in China, quickly reached different parts of the world, affecting people of all ages and backgrounds.

The spread of COVID-19 raised several questions and concerns about the feasibility and safety of hosting such a large-scale event. The Olympics, which traditionally bring together thousands of athletes and spectators from various countries, now had to consider the health implications of such a gathering. Discussions and deliberations took place among the organizers, health experts, and stakeholders about the best course of action. The situation highlighted the importance of adaptability and collaboration. The primary focus of the Olympics has always been on sports and competition, but the Tokyo 2020 Olympics brought to the forefront the need for global cooperation in addressing shared challenges. The world watched closely as decisions were made, showcasing the delicate balance between celebrating human achievements in sports and ensuring the well-being of all participants and attendees. In the end, the Tokyo 2020 Olympics served as a reminder of the interconnectedness of our global community. It emphasized that while sports can bring joy and inspiration, the health and safety of individuals remain paramount. The event also underscored the role of technology and innovation in addressing unforeseen challenges and ensuring that the spirit of the Games continues, even in the face of adversity.

Originating in Wuhan, China, in late 2019, COVID-19 rapidly spread across continents, leaving a trail of devastation in its wake. It wasn't just a virus; it was a highly contagious pathogen that attacked the respiratory system, leading to severe illness and, in many cases, death. Hospitals were overwhelmed, economies faltered, and daily life as we knew it came to a grinding halt. The bustling streets of major cities turned eerily quiet, iconic landmarks stood empty, and the collective heartbeat of humanity seemed to pause, waiting, watching, and hoping through a new reality of "social distancing."

Amidst this backdrop, the Tokyo Olympics faced a dilemma of historic proportions. The very ethos of the Games, bringing together athletes from every corner of the globe to congregate, compete, and celebrate, was now a potential recipe for disaster. The Olympic Village, usually a hub of camaraderie and cultural exchange, risked becoming a hotspot for viral transmission. The stadiums, where cheers and applause would typically reverberate, were faced with the prospect of silence or, at best, a smattering of applause from a limited audience. The juxtaposition was stark: the Olympics, a symbol of global unity and the pinnacle of athletic achievement, versus COVID-19, a grim reminder of our vulnerabilities and the interconnectedness of our world. The Games, which had always been an escape from global crises, were now at the epicenter of one that even it could not escape. If history has taught us anything, it's that adversity often breeds innovation. The challenges posed by COVID-19 were unprecedented, but they also presented an opportunity. As the world grappled with this new reality, it also began to adapt. The initial shock and despair gave way to resilience and innovation. And while COVID-19 had disrupted the traditional fabric of the Olympics, it also set the stage for a reimagining of the Games, which would lean heavily on technology and the collective human spirit never to give up and navigate the challenges ahead.

As the International Olympic Committee (IOC) grappled with decisions that would shape the future of the Games, technology emerged as the beacon, guiding the way through uncharted waters and delivering an opportunity for the world of sports to adapt, evolve, and lean on technology like never before. The Tokyo Olympics, originally envisioned as a testament to human achievement in sports, transformed into a testament to human resilience, adaptability, and the power of technological innovation. Over the years, the Olympics have faced numerous challenges, from political boycotts to security threats. However, the decision to postpone the Tokyo 2020 Olympics marked a unique and unprecedented moment in Olympic history.

As the world grappled with the escalating COVID-19 crisis, the IOC found itself in uncharted waters. The rapid spread of the virus, coupled with its severe health implications, raised significant concerns about the safety of athletes, officials, and spectators. By early 2020, as countries implemented lockdown measures and international travel came to a near standstill, the feasibility of hosting a global event of the Olympics' magnitude became increasingly uncertain. In March 2020, after intense deliberations and consultations with various stakeholders, the IOC made the momentous decision to postpone the Tokyo Olympics to 2021. The significance of this postponement cannot be overstated. The Olympics have been canceled three times in the past due to world wars, but this was the first-ever postponement of the Games in peacetime. The decision highlighted the global scale of the COVID-19 crisis and its profound impact on every facet of human life, including sports.

This decision came less than 48 hours after the IOC had initially given itself a four-week window to assess the situation. The swift turnaround underscored the gravity of the situation and the urgency to prioritize the health and safety of all involved. On March 24, 2020, the president of the IOC, Thomas Bach, and the prime minister of Japan, Shinzo Abe, issued a joint statement regarding the postponement of the Tokyo 2020 Olympics:

> **In the present circumstances and based on the information provided by WHO [World Health Organization] today, the IOC President and the Prime Minister of Japan have concluded that the Games of the XXXII Olympiad in Tokyo must be rescheduled to a**

> date beyond 2020 but not later than summer 2021, to safeguard
> the health of the athletes, everybody involved in the Olympic
> Games, and the international community.
>
> The leaders agreed that the Olympic Games in Tokyo could stand
> as a beacon of hope to the world during these troubled times and
> that the Olympic flame could become a light at the end of the
> tunnel in which the world finds itself at present. Therefore, it was
> agreed that the Olympic flame will stay in Japan. It was also agreed
> that the Games will keep the name Olympic and Paralympic Games
> Tokyo 2020.

The ramifications of this decision were felt far and wide. Athletes who had trained for years, aiming for peak performance in 2020, faced emotional and physical challenges as they recalibrated their training schedules. Japan, which had invested significant resources in infrastructure and logistics, grappled with the economic implications. Fans, who had eagerly anticipated the Games, faced disappointment, albeit tempered by the understanding of the larger global crisis at hand.

The Tokyo 2020 postponement stands out as a defining moment of Olympic history represents a stark departure from the norm and a symbol of the times we lived in. For more than a century, the Olympics have been a beacon of hope, a celebration of human potential, and a testament to the power of unity and competition. They have weathered political boycotts, economic downturns, and even global conflicts. Yet, they have always emerged, time and again, as a symbol of global unity. The decision to postpone the Tokyo 2020 Olympics was not taken lightly. It was a decision fraught with complexities, both logistical and emotional. But at its core, it was a decision that underscored a governing truth about the Olympic movement: its unwavering commitment to the well-being of its participants and spectators. The Tokyo 2020 postponement serves as a powerful testament to the Olympic spirit's resilience. It reminds us that the Games are more than just a collection of sporting events, medals, and ceremonies. They're about people. They're about athletes who dedicate their lives to their craft, fans who travel across the world to support their nations, and communities that come together to celebrate the best of humanity. In the face of a global crisis, the IOC chose to prioritize the health and safety of these individuals, even if it meant making an unprecedented decision.

The unprecedented event in the face of a pandemic serves as a poignant reminder of the delicate balance between celebrating human achievement and ensuring human well-being. Sports, in all their glory, reflect our shared human experience. They showcase our strengths, our vulnerabilities, our triumphs, and our defeats. They provide a platform for athletes to push the boundaries of what's possible, but they also carry a responsibility to protect and nurture the very individuals who make these feats possible. In years to come, the Tokyo 2020 Olympics will be remembered not just for the challenges it faced but for the values it upheld. It will be remembered as an Olympics that stood firm in its commitment to humanity, even in the face of adversity. It will be a testament to the idea that while sports can inspire and uplift, they must always, first and foremost, prioritize the well-being of the people at their heart.

When the Tokyo 2020 Olympics did get underway on July 23, 2021, with some preliminary events beginning on July 21, 2021, ensuring the well-being of all 11,420 athletes and their support teams representing 206 nations (including the Refugee Olympic Team and the Russian Olympic Committee) was of paramount importance. During the COVID-19 pandemic, the world quickly realized the importance of early detection and isolation of infected individuals to prevent the spread of the virus. One of the most effective tools in this endeavor was contact tracing, a method used to identify and notify individuals who may have come into close contact with an infected person. Contact tracing, while not a new concept, gained global adoption during the pandemic. At its core, it's a simple idea: track the interactions of an infected individual to identify potential chains of transmission. By doing so, health officials can quickly isolate and test those at risk, breaking the chain and preventing further spread. For an event as massive and globally interconnected as the Olympics, the importance of robust contact tracing cannot be overstated.

With athletes, coaches, officials, and staff arriving from all corners of the world, the potential for a localized outbreak to become a global superspreader event was a real and present danger. To address this, the Tokyo 2020 organizers employed a range of digital tools to bolster their contact tracing efforts. One such tool was the COCOA app, primarily used for contact tracing during the Games. The COCOA app, which stands for "COVID-19 Contact-Confirming Application," was developed under the guidance of the Japanese government. COCOA was one of the primary tools employed to ensure the safety of everyone involved in the Tokyo 2020 Olympics. Deployed as a smartphone application, COCOA was designed to assist in the rapid identification and notification of individuals who may have been in close proximity to a person who had tested positive for COVID-19. Utilizing Bluetooth technology, the app anonymously logs interactions between users, ensuring privacy while still maintaining a record of potential contacts. For the Tokyo 2020 Olympics, all participants, including athletes, officials, and staff, were encouraged to download and actively use the COCOA app. The app would run in the background, silently logging interactions without accessing personal data or location information. If a user tested positive for COVID-19, the app would send out notifications to those who had been in close contact with the infected individual, advising them to get tested and take necessary precautions.

This app, alongside other health reporting tools, played a pivotal role in monitoring interactions and potential exposures during the Games. Its real-time alert system allowed swift action, minimizing the risk of widespread outbreaks within the Olympic community. For instance, if an athlete or staff member tested positive, the app's data could be used to quickly identify and notify those who had been in close proximity, ensuring rapid testing and isolation. This swift response prevented potential outbreaks within the Olympic village and competition venues, ensuring the safety of all participants. However, it's essential to note that although COCOA was a valuable tool, it was just one part of a broader strategy. The app's effectiveness was maximized when combined with other measures like regular testing, masks, and social distancing.

Like all tools, COCOA was not without its challenges and criticisms. Concerns were raised about the app's accuracy, potential false positives, and the overall reliance on individuals to download and use the app correctly. Some also voiced concerns about data privacy, even though the app was designed to prioritize user anonymity. The app represented a fusion of technology and public health, showcasing how digital tools can be harnessed to tackle real-world challenges. The app's role in the Tokyo 2020 Olympics serves as a testament to the potential of technology to safeguard public health, especially in large-scale international events. Yet, despite these challenges, the digital shield of contact tracing undeniably played a pivotal role in the successful hosting of the Tokyo 2020 Olympics. It showcased the potential of technology to safeguard public health, even in the most complex and challenging of circumstances.

In a world suddenly thrust into isolation by the COVID-19 pandemic, the fundamental basics of how humans were able to interact underwent a seismic shift. Traditional face-to-face meetings, training sessions, and even casual interactions became potential health risks. This posed a unique challenge for the Tokyo 2020 Olympics, an event that thrives on global collaboration, intense training, and meticulous planning. Historically, the IOC has been synonymous with grandeur and tradition. Its assemblies, often held in iconic venues, were a blend of ceremonial rituals and crucial decision-making. Press conferences were bustling events, filled with journalists, cameras, and the palpable energy of anticipation. Coordination meetings, essential to the seamless execution of the Games, were typically face-to-face, fostering direct communication and collaboration. However, the COVID-19 pandemic necessitated a new way of thinking and a completely different approach. The grand halls and packed press rooms were no longer viable, replaced instead by the virtual realm.

The IOC, faced with the unprecedented challenges brought about by the pandemic, demonstrated remarkable adaptability by swiftly transitioning to digital platforms for their operations. Platforms such as Zoom, Microsoft Teams, and Skype, which were previously considered secondary or backup tools suddenly became the lifeline of their communication and coordination efforts. These digital tools not only provided a means to communicate but also introduced features that mirrored, and at times surpassed, the functionalities of traditional face-to-face meetings. The availability of breakout rooms facilitated focused group discussions, screen sharing enabled seamless presentations, and real-time polls provided instant feedback, fostering a dynamic and interactive environment.

With international travel becoming increasingly restricted and health advisories cautioning against large gatherings, the usual bustling and interactive physical meetings became a thing of the past. The new norm was logging in virtually. IOC members, delegates, organizers, and stakeholders, irrespective of their geographical locations, could now participate from the comfort and safety of their homes or workspaces. This not only ensured that the meticulous planning and coordination for the Games continued without interruption but also introduced an element of flexibility and convenience. The inherent advantages of these digital platforms, such as eliminating travel time and the ability to schedule back-to-back sessions, meant that the frequency of meetings could be increased if the situation demanded. This was particularly beneficial in an environment where developments were unfolding rapidly and decisions had to be made on the fly. In essence, the IOC's proactive embrace of technology ensured that, despite the challenges, the spirit of collaboration, planning, and progress remained undeterred.

The media, an integral part of the Olympic experience, also had to adapt to this new COVID-19 world. Traditional press conferences, with their packed rooms and live interactions, posed a health risk. In response to this, the IOC began streaming press conferences online. Journalists could attend virtually, ask questions in real time, and even conduct one-on-one interviews through breakout rooms. This approach not only ensured safety but also democratized access. Reporters from around the world, who might not have had the resources to travel, could now participate, broadening the global reach and inclusivity of the event. The IOC's swift adaptation to digital platforms was not just a response to a crisis; it was a forward-looking approach that recognized the evolving nature of communication and collaboration. The circumstances that prompted this shift were challenging, but the outcomes showcased the potential of technology to bridge gaps, foster unity, and ensure the continuity of tradition in the modern age.

The pandemic presented a unique set of challenges for athletes, who are accustomed to rigorous training routines, team interactions, and global competitions. Suddenly, they found themselves confined, their usual training grounds inaccessible, and their support systems limited by distance. Maintaining peak physical condition became a complex task. Traditional training facilities, from gyms to tracks to pools, were often closed or restricted. Athletes had to innovate, turning their living spaces into makeshift training areas. However, physical training is as much about guidance and feedback as it is about exercise. To bridge this gap, many athletes turned to virtual training tools and apps.

In the digital age, a massive number of platforms have emerged, offering a laundry list of features tailored to the needs of athletes. These range from tracking intricate fitness metrics to facilitating comprehensive virtual coaching sessions. Notable examples include Fitbit and WHOOP, which have revolutionized the way athletes receive feedback. With these tools, coaches can provide real-time insights and adjustments to their trainees, irrespective of the vast geographical distances that might separate them. This ensures that training programs are not only effective but also customized to cater to the unique requirements of each athlete. Wearable technology has come to the forefront of this digital transformation in sports. Its importance was underscored during the pandemic when traditional training facilities were shuttered. A prime example was the English Premier League's strategic use of wearables. They employed these devices to monitor their players' fitness closely and performance metrics during remote training sessions, a necessity during the nationwide lockdowns.

Furthermore, platforms designed for real-time coaching have bridged the gap between athletes and their mentors. One such platform, Coach-Now, stands out for its comprehensive offerings. CoachNow provides a comprehensive ecosystem that supports the entire coaching process.

Its capabilities extend beyond basic communication. The platform offers state-of-the-art video analysis, allowing coaches to review and break down an athlete's performance frame by frame. This, combined with the provision for instant feedback, ensures that athletes receive timely and actionable insights into their techniques and strategies. Moreover, the platform's emphasis on continuous communication fosters a collaborative environment where athletes and coaches can engage in productive discussions, share resources, and set goals. In essence, with platforms like CoachNow, the coaching realm has been redefined. Remote coaching, once seen as a challenge, is now viewed as an efficient and effective approach, ensuring that athletes receive consistent guidance and support, regardless of where they or their coaches are located.

The challenges brought about by the COVID-19 pandemic were undeniably daunting. However, they also served as a catalyst, fast-tracking the integration of technology in the world of sports and fitness. These digital tools and platforms were instrumental in ensuring that athletes could continue their rigorous training routines, introducing them to novel methods of monitoring, training, and enhancing their performance. This fusion of sports and technology stands as a shining example of human ingenuity, adaptability, and the unwavering commitment to achieving excellence, even when confronted with unprecedented challenges.

In the midst of the pandemic, ensuring the health and safety of everyone involved in the Tokyo 2020 Olympics was paramount. Traditional methods of sanitization, though effective, were labor intensive and couldn't guarantee consistent coverage, especially in vast areas like stadiums and training facilities. Enter the age of robotic sanitization. As the world grappled with the pandemic, technology once again stepped up to offer solutions. Robots equipped with UV lights, disinfectant sprayers, and advanced sensors began to make their mark in various sectors, from hospitals to airports. The Tokyo 2020 Olympics embraced this technology wholeheartedly. These robots, designed to navigate complex environments, were deployed across various Olympic venues, ensuring thorough and consistent disinfection. The primary role of these sanitization robots was to maintain a COVID-free environment. They operated during off-hours in stadiums, meticulously covering every inch of the seating areas, corridors, and locker rooms. In the Olympic Village and training facilities, they worked in tandem with cleaning crews, ensuring that areas frequently touched by athletes and staff, such as doorknobs, railings, and equipment, were regularly disinfected. Their efficiency was not just in their thoroughness but also in their speed. What would take a team of humans hours to clean could be achieved by robots in a fraction of the time, ensuring that facilities are ready to use with minimal downtime.

The Tokyo Olympics saw the debut of robotic custodians, a sight that was both novel and intriguing for many. Their presence elicited a range of reactions from athletes and staff alike. For many, seeing these robots in action was a testament to the lengths the organizers were willing to go to ensure the highest standards of hygiene and safety. Athletes, coaches, and other personnel expressed a palpable sense of relief, comforted by the knowledge that their training and competition spaces were being meticulously sanitized. Interestingly, the robots also became somewhat of a social media sensation. Athletes, particularly those hailing from countries with a penchant for technology, were captivated by these mechanical marvels. Social media platforms were abuzz with videos and posts showcasing the sanitization robots diligently performing their tasks, often accompanied by captions reflecting awe and admiration.

However, as with any significant change, there were a few dissenting voices. Concerns were raised about the potential implications of such technology on employment, with some fearing that robots might eventually supplant human roles, especially in areas traditionally reliant on the human touch. The Olympics, after all, is as much about human connection and shared experiences as it is about competition. However, the prevailing sentiment leaned toward gratitude. In an era marked by unpredictability and apprehension due to the pandemic, these robots emerged as beacons of reassurance. They allowed athletes, coaches, and staff to focus their energies solely on the Games, alleviating concerns about health risks.

The Tokyo 2020 Olympics beautifully encapsulated the harmonious blend of age-old traditions with cutting-edge technology, mirroring Japan's journey as a nation. The heart and soul of the Games remained deeply rooted in its time-honored values, but the methods adopted to ensure the well-being of its participants underwent a transformative evolution. The sanitization robots, with their unwavering dedication and precision, epitomized this metamorphosis. They stood as silent sentinels, guardians of health, ensuring the Olympic spirit thrived in a safe and secure environment.

Although the Olympics had been broadcast worldwide for decades, the Tokyo 2020 Olympics took digital engagement to new heights. With travel restrictions in place and limited in-person attendance, there was a pressing need to ensure that fans across the globe could experience the magic of the Games. Technology rose to the occasion, bridging the gap between the event and its global audience. In the world of sports broadcasting, the Tokyo 2020 Olympics marked a significant leap forward, harnessing the power of cutting-edge technologies to deliver an unparalleled viewing experience. The essence of the Games, with its high-octane performances and raw emotions, was captured with a precision and clarity that was nothing short of revolutionary. The Tokyo 2020 Olympics underscored a vital message: geographical boundaries are becoming increasingly irrelevant. With high-speed Internet, advanced streaming technologies, and digital platforms, the Games were accessible to anyone with a screen and a connection, from bustling cities to remote villages. This democratization of access ensures that the spirit of the Olympics and its ethos of unity, competition, and celebration resonate globally.

The deployment of advanced high-definition cameras was a game-changer. With their ability to capture minute details, these cameras ensured that viewers didn't miss a single bead of sweat, a fleeting expression, or a rapid movement. Slow-motion replays, enabled by these cameras, allowed fans to relive crucial moments, dissecting every move of their favorite athletes. Complementing the visual experience was an immersive sound system that replicated the ambiance of the stadium. Even with limited live audiences, microphones strategically placed around the venues picked up every cheer, every shout, and even the rhythmic breathing of competitors, creating a surround sound experience for viewers at home.

The Tokyo 2020 Olympics wasn't just about passive viewing; it was about immersion. Augmented reality (AR) platforms provided fans with interactive overlays, offering real-time statistics, athlete bios, and even trivia. This added layer of information enriched the viewing experience, making it both entertaining and informative. Virtual reality (VR), on the other hand, was all about transporting fans to the heart of the action. Using platforms like Intel's True VR, which boasted features like 8K definition and a 360-degree view, fans could virtually place themselves in the stadium. Whether it was feeling the rush of a 100-meter sprint or the tension of a penalty shootout, VR ensured that fans were not just spectators but part of the event. The role of streaming platforms and digital media was pivotal. Traditional broadcasting was complemented by platforms like YouTube, Twitch, and various sports-specific streaming services. These platforms cater to the modern viewer, offering flexibility in viewing times, interactive features, and tailored content. Social media played its part, too. Platforms like Twitter, Instagram, and Facebook became hubs for real-time updates, athlete interactions, and fan discussions.

Memorable moments became viral sensations within minutes, ensuring even those unfamiliar with a particular sport could partake in its most iconic moments. Tokyo didn't just set a new standard for sports broadcasting; it provided a vision of what's to come—a future where fans are deeply connected to the action, where the thrill of the game is a shared global experience, and where technology acts as the bridge between the athlete and the audience. The Games have always been a celebration of human potential, and with these technological strides, they promise to be an even more inclusive and exhilarating spectacle in the years to come.

The Tokyo 2020 Olympics also marked a significant leap in the utilization of digital twin technology, a concept that has been gaining traction across various industries. Digital twins are essentially virtual replicas of physical entities, allowing for real-time simulations and analyses of various scenarios. In the context of the Olympics, this technology was harnessed to optimize the planning and execution of events, ensuring a seamless and enhanced experience for athletes, organizers, and spectators alike. Digital twinning was employed to create accurate virtual representations of key competition venues. These digital replicas allowed organizers to simulate changes in real time, offering insights into how modifications to a venue might impact factors such as lighting, audio quality, and crowd movement. For instance, they could determine the optimal placements for barriers, fencing, vehicles, teams, and volunteers. Additionally, they could identify the best camera positions to enhance TV coverage quality. This technology was not just about planning; it was about optimizing the experience for everyone involved. Beyond the logistical benefits, digital twins also played a role in enhancing the spectator experience. With these virtual replicas, spectators could virtually navigate the Olympic venues, getting a feel for the environment even before they physically arrived. This was particularly beneficial for those with disabilities, allowing for better accessibility planning. The technology facilitated greater collaboration among various stakeholders. Since these digital models were remotely accessible, there was enhanced coordination between the IOC, broadcast teams, international federations, and suppliers. This not only streamlined the planning process but also reduced the need for physical site visits, leading to a decrease in emissions and underscoring the sustainability aspect of the Games. The 2020 Olympics showcased the great potential that digital twins can play in revolutionizing the way large-scale events are planned and executed. Creating a bridge between the virtual and physical worlds, this technology ensured that the Olympics were not just an event to watch but an experience to be lived, regardless of a person's location. As we look to the future, it's evident that digital twins will play an even more integral role in shaping the evolution of sports events, making them more inclusive, efficient, and immersive.

In the shadow of the COVID-19 pandemic, the Tokyo 2020 Olympics emerged as a symbol of unparalleled resilience, unity, and hope. As nations grappled with the pandemic's ramifications, the very feasibility of hosting such a monumental event came under scrutiny. The decision to postpone the Olympics, a move unheard of in peacetime, underscored the gravity of the situation and the collective responsibility to prioritize global health. However, amidst this backdrop of uncertainty and adversity, the Games emerged as a beacon of human tenacity and the power of collective spirit. They served as a poignant reminder that with innovation, adaptability, and a shared vision, even the most formidable challenges can be transformed into opportunities for growth and unity. The athletic feats were undeniably awe-inspiring, but the true essence of these Olympics lay in its celebration of global togetherness, mutual support, and the unwavering determination of humanity to rise above even the most daunting obstacles. The role of technology in making the Tokyo Games a resounding success cannot be overstated. From advanced broadcasting methods that brought the events to every corner of the globe to VR experiences that immersed fans in the heart of the action to digital tools that ensured the safety and well-being of athletes and staff, technology was the linchpin that held the Games together. It facilitated adaptability in the face of changing circumstances, ensured seamless communication amidst travel restrictions, and, most importantly, provided mechanisms to prioritize health and safety without compromising the spirit of competition.

Beyond the athletic achievements and the technological innovations, the Tokyo 2020 Olympics will be cherished for its broader, more profound implications. It underscored the pivotal role of collaboration, innovation, and vision in navigating challenges. The Games demonstrated that when technology is employed with purpose and foresight, it has the transformative power to uplift, connect, and inspire humanity. In the rich records of Olympic history, Tokyo 2020 will occupy a place of honor, not just for the medals clinched or records set but for its enduring legacy of hope and determination. It stands as a testament to the world's collective strength in the face of adversity, reminding us of the boundless potential that arises when we unite in purpose and spirit. The Tokyo Games serves as a beacon for future global events, illustrating that with the right blend of innovation, collaboration, and human resilience, the Olympic flame will continue to shine brightly, illuminating the path for future generations and inspiring them to reach ever greater heights.

CHAPTER 10

Green Technologies and Climate and Sustainability Initiatives

The Beijing 2022 Winter Olympics

Beijing, a city that has already etched its name in the annals of Olympic history, once again took center stage on February 4, 2022. The world watched in awe as the Chinese capital became the first city to host both the Summer and Winter Olympic Games. But this time, the spectacle was not just about athletic prowess or international unity; it was a statement about sustainability, a blueprint for future Games to be as green as the emblematic Olympic rings. The Opening Ceremony of the 2022 Games was created as a symphony of sustainability. As the torchbearers, Dinigeer Yilamujiang and Zhao Jiawen ascended the steps of the National Stadium, the air was alive and filled with anticipation, but not with carbon emissions. The duo, both Millennials, were not just carrying the Olympic flame; they were carrying the hopes of a planet in dire need of environmental stewardship. The snowflake-shaped cauldron that awaited served not only as a piece of art, but also as a symbol of China's commitment to making these Winter Olympics a green affair. The cauldron, an intricate design made up of smaller snowflakes, represented the 91 delegations participating in the Games. As Yilamujiang and Jiawen placed the torch in the center of this giant snowflake, it rotated upward, transforming into the Olympic cauldron. Breaking from tradition, and Olympic history, the flame was tiny, yet it spoke volumes. This was a flame reimagined.

Zhang Yimou, the renowned Chinese filmmaker responsible for the opening and closing ceremonies, revealed that this tiny flame was a deliberate choice inspired by the principles of low-carbon development and environmental protection. Unlike previous Games, which used liquefied natural gas or propane to fuel the Olympic torch, Beijing 2022 broke new ground by using hydrogen energy. When burned, hydrogen produces only water, emitting zero carbon dioxide. This was an amazing technological feat, and it was a statement, a vision of a sustainable future that could be realized if the world came together, much like the athletes in the stadium. The night sky over the National Stadium was lit up with fireworks displays only three times during the Opening Ceremony, for a total of just three minutes. Cai Guoqiang, the chief visual art designer, explained that the fireworks were specially designed to be environmentally friendly. Developed in Hunan and Hebei provinces, these fireworks were made with nontoxic gunpowder and produced no smoke. Even in their brevity and composition, the fireworks were a nod to the Games' overarching theme of environmental responsibility. Zhang Yimou emphasized that the restrained use of fireworks was a conscious decision to minimize environmental impact. "This indicates our confidence in our culture," he said. It was as if China was saying, "We don't need to shout to be heard." The message was clear: sustainability is not just a policy, it's a culture, a way of life that needs to be integrated into every aspect of our existence, including sports.

While the Olympic athletes were locked in their own battles, pushing the boundaries of human capability, striving for that elusive gold medal, and navigating the pressures of representing their countries on the world stage, the event organizers were engaged in a different but equally formidable challenge. They were grappling with the monumental task of making the Beijing 2022 Winter Olympics the most sustainable Games ever held. This wasn't just about checking boxes or meeting quotas; it was about fundamentally rethinking how a global event of this magnitude could coexist with the planet's ecological needs. This intricate dance between athletic excellence and environmental responsibility forms what has come to be known as the *sustainability paradox*—the apparent contradiction between the pursuit of economic growth and the need to protect the environment and ensure social well-being. The sustainability paradox arises from the challenge of balancing the achievement of good financial results with the integration of social and environmental considerations.

On one hand, there was an unyielding commitment to green initiatives during the 2022 Games, a dedication to renewable energy, waste management, and water conservation that was nothing short of groundbreaking. On the other hand, this noble pursuit was fraught with complexities and ethical dilemmas that challenged the very essence of what it means to be sustainable. This paradox isn't hidden away as a footnote in the annals of Olympic history—it's a vivid, compelling narrative that underscores the intricate, often conflicting variables that come into play when we aim to reconcile human ambition with the imperatives of ecological stewardship. It serves as both a cautionary tale and a source of inspiration, a real-world case study that lays bare the challenges and opportunities inherent in the global push for sustainability.

Beijing's commitment to hosting an eco-friendly Winter Olympics was nothing short of Herculean. The city aimed to set a new standard for sustainability, and in many ways, it succeeded. The use of renewable energy was a cornerstone of this effort. Solar panels adorned the roofs of Olympic venues, capturing the sun's energy to power everything from lighting to heating systems. In 2022, the world was becoming increasingly aware of the perils of climate change. The Winter Games focused on solar power as a cornerstone of their sustainability strategy. The organizers made a concerted effort to integrate solar panels into the infrastructure of all Olympic venues. This was integrated into their strategy and planning as a fundamental design principle. From the ski slopes to the ice rinks, solar panels were strategically placed to maximize energy capture, converting the abundant sunlight into usable electricity. These solar installations served multiple purposes. First, they substantially reduced the Games' carbon footprint, aligning with global efforts to combat climate change. Second, they set a powerful precedent for future Olympic Games and large-scale sporting events. By successfully implementing solar technology on such a grand stage, the Beijing Winter Olympics demonstrated that renewable energy could meet the demands of even the most logistically complex events.

The Olympic Village stood as a beacon of sustainable design and innovation. The Village became so much more than a place for athletes to rest and prepare for their events; it was a living, breathing example of what can be achieved when sustainability is prioritized. Solar panels were seamlessly integrated into the architectural design of the buildings, almost as if they were an aesthetic feature rather than a functional one. But make no mistake, these panels were workhorses. The solar installations at the Olympic Village served a multitude of functions. They powered the heating systems, ensuring that athletes could enjoy a warm and comfortable environment. They provided electricity for lighting, both indoor and outdoor, reducing the need for conventional energy sources. They even contributed to powering the various electronic systems and amenities within the village, from the gyms to the dining halls. This initiative had ripple effects beyond the immediate context of the Games. By significantly reducing energy costs, the solar-powered Olympic Village became a case study in economic and environmental sustainability. Moreover, it aligned perfectly with China's broader goals of reducing carbon emissions and transitioning to renewable energy sources. In essence, the solar initiatives at the Beijing 2022 Winter Olympics were far more than a one-off project. They were a statement, a vision of what the future could look like when we harness the power of the sun for the greater good. And in doing so, they elevated the discourse on sustainability from mere talk to actionable results.

Wind turbines also played a key role in providing clean power to the Winter Games. As part of the event's broader sustainability strategy, the turbines played a pivotal role in powering the Games, particularly in key venues. Besides being a nod to environmental consciousness, it was a full-scale operational maneuver that demonstrated the viability of renewable energy in large-scale events. The wind turbines weren't randomly placed throughout the Olympic site for show, they were strategically located near key venues to maximize their contribution to the overall energy mix. Engineers and planners conducted extensive studies to identify the most effective locations for these turbines. They considered factors like wind speed, direction, and consistency, as well as the proximity to the electrical grid and the venues themselves. The result was an optimized setup that not only generated enough power to provide energy to the Games but did so efficiently and reliably.

Perhaps the most compelling example of wind energy's impact was its role in powering the ice rinks. Ice rinks are notorious energy hogs. Maintaining the optimal conditions for competitive ice sports, including figure skating, ice hockey, and speed skating, requires a significant amount of energy. The cooling systems must work around the clock to keep the ice at the perfect temperature and consistency. In addition to the cooling needs for the ice, lighting, sound systems, and other electrical needs must also be met. In Beijing, wind energy was the primary source of power for these rinks. This calculated, innovative approach achieved a significant reduction in the carbon footprint of the Games. By using wind energy, the organizers were able to cut down on greenhouse gas emissions, thereby making a strong statement about the potential of renewable energy in large-scale operations. According to post-Games data, the wind turbines contributed to a significant percentage of the total energy consumed during the Games. The use of wind energy reduced the need for fossil fuels, which are traditionally used in such large-scale events. This not only lowered carbon emissions but also set a precedent for future events to follow. The success of this initiative has had far-reaching implications. It serves as a case study for other large-scale events, from music festivals to World Cups, on how to integrate renewable energy sources effectively. Moreover, it provides a blueprint for cities and countries looking to make a transition to more sustainable energy solutions.

Often, when we think of the Olympics, we mostly focus on the athletes, the competitions, and the medals. But what about the unsung heroes who make these events possible? No, I'm not talking about the coaches or the volunteers, although they're crucial, too. I'm talking about the innovative technologies that power the Games—specifically, geothermal energy. This renewable energy source was a key player in the Olympic facilities, providing efficient heating solutions that were as eco-friendly as they were effective. Geothermal energy is essentially heat derived from the Earth's core. By tapping into this natural resource, the Olympic organizers were able to maintain a comfortable indoor environment across various facilities. This wasn't simply an effort in providing comfort for those on the ground at the Winter Games, it was about creating a sustainable infrastructure that could meet the demands of a large-scale event without compromising on environmental responsibility.

One area where geothermal energy was used to great success was the Olympic Village. The Village served as a microcosm of international talent and a hub of activity during the Games. Keeping athletes warm and comfortable is not just a matter of convenience; it's a necessity for peak performance. To achieve this, a state-of-the-art geothermal heating system was installed, replacing traditional heating methods that often rely on fossil fuels. The system worked by circulating a specialized fluid, often a mixture of water and antifreeze, through a series of underground pipes. These pipes were buried deep enough to reach stable thermal zones where the Earth's natural heat is more consistent. As the fluid traveled through this subterranean network, it absorbed the Earth's natural heat. When the fluid was sufficiently heated, it was then pumped back to the surface and circulated throughout the Olympic Village. This process effectively distributed a comfortable, consistent level of warmth, all while leveraging a renewable energy source that has a minimal impact on the environment. The result? A consistent, comfortable temperature that required significantly less energy to maintain. This case study serves as a shining example of how geothermal energy can be effectively harnessed for large-scale applications, offering a sustainable solution that doesn't sacrifice efficiency. According to data provided by the United Nations Environment Programme, the geothermal heating system, as well as other methods used throughout the Beijing 2022 Olympics reduced energy consumption by a notable margin compared to traditional heating methods. This is a big deal, especially when you consider the scale of the event and the number of facilities involved. The reduction in energy usage translated into lower carbon emissions, contributing to the overall sustainability goals of the Games.

The use of geothermal energy was part of a larger sustainability strategy that also included eco-friendly building materials. From recycled steel to sustainably sourced wood, the construction of the Olympic venues was a master class in environmental responsibility. These materials not only reduced the carbon footprint of the construction process but also complemented the geothermal systems, creating a synergy of sustainability. The construction teams worked closely with environmental experts to select materials that would not only meet structural requirements but also align with sustainability goals. This multifaceted approach ensured that environmental impact was minimized at every stage, from planning to execution. The successful implementation of geothermal energy at the Olympics serves as a blueprint for other large-scale events and even for cities looking to transition to more sustainable energy solutions. It's a compelling proof of concept that shows what's possible when we look beyond traditional methods and tap into the Earth's resources. The decision to implement geothermal energy at the 2022 Winter Olympics delivered a very strong message to the rest of the world: a commitment to sustainability that went beyond mere words. By harnessing the Earth's natural heat, the organizers not only provided a comfortable environment for athletes and spectators alike but also set a new standard for what large-scale events can achieve in terms of environmental responsibility. As we look to the future, the role of geothermal energy in these Games serves as a powerful example, a playbook, if you will, of how to integrate sustainability into every facet of our lives.

However, as with any monumental and innovative endeavor, the road to sustainability was not without its bumps and turns. The construction of new infrastructure, for instance, was a double-edged sword. The buildings were designed with eco-friendly materials and energy-efficient systems, but their very existence required significant natural resources, concrete, steel, and timber. Each had its own environmental cost, and the balance sheet was not always in Mother Nature's favor. Then there's the elephant in the room: carbon emissions from international travel.

Athletes, officials, media, and fans flew in from all corners of the globe, their journeys powered by fossil fuels. The irony was on full public display. An event striving for environmental excellence was also a catalyst for carbon emissions on a global scale. Let's not forget the controversial artificial snow. Although it reduced the need for natural snow and the associated water usage, it wasn't without its ethical dilemmas. The production of artificial snow still requires water, which was often sourced from local reservoirs, impacting the surrounding ecosystems. In addition to the impact on the local water ecosystem, the chemicals used in the snow-making process raised concerns about long-term environmental effects.

The use of manufactured snow, created by snow cannons that spray water droplets into the cold air, was a contentious issue leading up to and during the Beijing Winter Olympics. Critics argued that it was an energy-intensive process that contradicted the Games' sustainability goals. However, proponents pointed out that climate change has made natural snowfall less reliable, necessitating technological interventions to ensure the Games could proceed. One of the key sustainability aspects was the water source used for snowmaking. The Beijing Winter Olympics utilized recycled water, reducing the demand for local freshwater resources. Advances in snowmaking technology have made the process more energy-efficient than in the past. Modern snow cannons, for example, can produce more snow per gallon of water and per kilowatt-hour of energy. In an era of climate unpredictability, manufactured snow can be seen as an adaptive strategy. It allows winter sports to continue in regions where natural snowfall has become less reliable, thereby spreading the economic benefits of hosting such events.

The athletes had mixed reactions to the manufactured snow. While some, like American alpine skier Mikaela Shiffrin, noted that the quality of manufactured snow can be more consistent, others missed the unique characteristics of natural snow. Norwegian cross-country skier Therese Johaug mentioned that natural snow provides a different kind of grip and glide, which can affect race strategies and outcomes. However, most athletes acknowledged the reality that climate change is affecting winter sports and expressed appreciation for the efforts to make the Games as sustainable as possible. Marie-Philip Poulin, the Canadian ice hockey player and environmental advocate, commented that while natural snow is preferable, the use of recycled water in snowmaking was a responsible approach given the circumstances. The use of manufactured snow at the Beijing 2022 Winter Olympics serves as a microcosm of the larger challenges and debates surrounding sustainability in sports. It's a complex issue that doesn't lend itself to easy answers. However, what is clear is that as the climate continues to change, the sports world will have to adapt, innovate, and sometimes make compromises to continue providing the spectacle and competition that captivates millions around the globe.

The use of sustainable timber in the construction of Olympic venues is a testament to the commitment to environmental responsibility. Sourcing timber from responsibly managed forests ensures a reduced carbon footprint and promotes sustainable forestry practices. Sustainably managed forests are also more biodiverse compared to forests that have been irresponsibly logged. Biodiversity is crucial for ecosystem resilience, which affects everything from local weather patterns to the habitats of endangered species. Sustainable timber is an environmental as well as an economic issue. Forests that are managed with long-term sustainability in mind are more likely to provide economic benefits for longer periods, supporting the livelihoods of local communities. This creates a virtuous cycle where economic benefits incentivize further sustainable practices.

In Beijing, the Olympic organizers partnered with certified suppliers to ensure that the timber used met stringent sustainability criteria. Sustainable timber is often locally sourced, reducing the energy required for transportation. Additionally, certified suppliers are more likely to use every part of the tree, reducing waste. In the case of the Beijing Winter Olympics, partnering with certified suppliers ensured that the timber used was both local and utilized efficiently, thereby minimizing waste and energy consumption. An example of where this was used to great effect was the ski jump, a marvel of engineering and design that was constructed primarily using sustainable timber. Not only did this choice reduce the overall carbon footprint of the venue, but it also showcased the aesthetic and functional capabilities of wood as a building material. Athletes like Norway's Maren Lundby, who clinched a gold medal in women's ski jumping, soared through the air against the backdrop of these eco-conscious structures, symbolizing the harmonious relationship between sports and sustainability. When a high-profile event like the Olympics commits to using sustainable timber, it sets a precedent for other large-scale events and construction projects. This has a ripple effect, encouraging more industries to adopt sustainable practices. It sends a powerful message that sustainability and economic development can go together, challenging the notion that environmental responsibility is at odds with progress.

Recycled materials have increasingly become a cornerstone in sustainable construction practices. The Beijing 2022 Winter Olympics took this to heart by incorporating recycled steel, plastic, and even concrete into the construction of its venues. One of the most immediate benefits of using recycled materials is the conservation of natural resources. Mining for new materials like steel and aluminum is both energy-intensive and environmentally damaging. By using recycled materials, we reduce the need for new resources, thereby conserving what's already available. The process of recycling materials generally consumes less energy than producing new materials from raw resources. For instance, recycling steel requires 60 percent less energy than producing steel from iron ore. This significant reduction in energy consumption translates to fewer greenhouse gas emissions, contributing to the fight against climate change. Construction waste accounts for a significant portion of landfill waste. By using recycled materials, we not only divert waste from landfills but also reduce the need for new landfills altogether. This has a cascading positive effect on soil conservation, groundwater quality, and even air quality. Recycled materials are often less expensive than new materials, offering economic incentives for sustainable construction. This cost-effectiveness can make large-scale projects more feasible and free up funds for other sustainability initiatives.

The Beijing Winter Olympics served as a high-profile example of how recycled materials can be effectively used in construction without compromising on quality or safety. The Olympic stadium, often referred to as the "Bird's Nest," featured an extensive use of recycled steel in its construction. This not only reduced the demand for new materials but also lowered the energy consumption associated with the production of new steel. The result was a structure that was both iconic and environmentally responsible, a fitting stage for athletes like American snowboarder Shaun White, who has always been vocal about climate change and sustainability. The event's global reach meant that this commitment to sustainability was broadcast to millions of people worldwide. By incorporating recycled steel, plastic, and concrete into its venues, the Beijing 2022 Winter Olympics set a new standard for future sporting events and construction projects. This sends a strong message to industries worldwide that sustainability is not just "nice-to-have" but a "must-have." Athletes who participated in the Games, many of whom have substantial followings, served as amplifiers for the sustainability message. When athletes like Shaun White compete in such venues, it adds another layer of credibility and urgency to the cause.

In addition to making use of recycled materials, insulation is a critical component in any structure, but it takes on added significance in a winter setting where energy efficiency is paramount. Traditional insulation materials can be effective but often come at a high environmental cost. Green insulation materials, on the other hand, are designed to provide excellent thermal performance while minimizing environmental impact. This is crucial for energy conservation, especially in winter sports venues where maintaining specific temperatures is nonnegotiable for the integrity of the Games. Materials like sheep's wool and recycled foam have a significantly lower carbon footprint compared to traditional insulation materials like fiberglass. Sheep's wool, for instance, is a renewable resource and can absorb and release moisture without compromising its insulating properties, making it highly efficient. While the initial investment in green insulation can be higher, the long-term savings in energy costs often offset this cost. Energy-efficient buildings are cheaper to run, reducing the overall operational costs of hosting large-scale events like the Olympics. Importantly, green insulation materials are often free from harmful chemicals and irritants, making them safer for both the construction workers who install them and the athletes and spectators who occupy the buildings. The Beijing Winter Olympics offered a global platform to showcase the effectiveness of green insulation. By using materials like sheep's wool and recycled foam, the event sent a clear message that sustainability and performance could go together. The ice arenas, where sports like figure skating and ice hockey captivated millions, were insulated using advanced, eco-friendly materials. These materials not only provided excellent thermal performance but also contributed to a significant reduction in energy costs for cooling the rinks. Athletes like Russian figure skater Kamila Valieva performed breathtaking routines in venues that were as committed to excellence in sustainability as they were in providing a stage for athletic prowess.

The Olympic venues serve as real-world case studies that architects, engineers, and policymakers can refer to when advocating for green insulation and energy efficiency in future projects. The data collected on energy savings and performance can provide compelling evidence to support further investment in these technologies. Athletes are increasingly becoming advocates for climate action and sustainability. When they compete in venues that prioritize these values, it adds weight to the broader message. When a venue as high-profile as an Olympic ice arena adopts green technologies, it sets a precedent for other venues around the world. This can have a ripple effect, encouraging more widespread adoption of sustainable practices in the construction and maintenance of sports facilities. For instance, athletes like Swedish ice hockey player Victor Olofsson, who has spoken about the importance of sustainability, lend their voices and platforms to amplify the message further.

Water is a multifaceted resource in the context of the Winter Olympic Games. It goes far beyond quenching thirst, it's about maintaining the ice for sports like hockey and figure skating, providing sanitation facilities for thousands of athletes and visitors, and even creating artificial snow when Mother Nature doesn't cooperate. The management of this resource is a logistical feat that requires meticulous planning and execution. In a world where water scarcity is becoming increasingly prevalent, the responsible management of this resource is not just an operational necessity but a moral imperative. According to the United Nations, by 2025, an estimated 1.8 billion people will live in areas plagued by water scarcity. This makes the conservation efforts of large-scale events like the Olympics even more critical, as they set the tone for what can be achieved on a global scale. One of the most innovative measures implemented at the Beijing 2022 Winter Olympics was rainwater harvesting. Specialized systems were installed to collect, filter, and store rainwater, which was then used for various purposes, including maintaining the quality of ice and snow at the venues. This not only reduced the demand for fresh water but also minimized the runoff that can lead to erosion and other environmental issues. Wastewater treatment is often a neglected aspect of water management, but it's crucial for both environmental sustainability and public health. The Beijing Winter Olympics employed advanced wastewater treatment technologies that not only met but exceeded international standards. These systems treated wastewater to a level where it could be safely reused for nonpotable purposes, such as landscape irrigation and toilet flushing, thereby creating a closed-loop system that minimized waste. For athletes, the quality of water can have a direct impact on their performance. Whether it's the quality of ice in a skating rink or the availability of clean water for hydration, effective water management is integral to the success of the Games.

Athletes like Canadian ice hockey player Marie-Philip Poulin's advocacy for environmental causes and her participation in a sustainably managed event like the Beijing 2022 Winter Olympics create a ripple effect. It encourages other athletes, fans, and even corporate sponsors to take notice and consider their environmental impact. This can lead to more athletes speaking out, more fans taking action, and more sponsors investing in sustainable practices. The Olympics provide a global platform, and athletes like Poulin use this platform to speak on issues that matter to them. When she praises the sustainability efforts of the Games, it's not just a passing comment; it's a statement that has the potential to inspire change. It validates the efforts of the organizers and sets a precedent for future events to aim for similar, if not better, sustainability standards.

The Beijing 2022 Winter Olympics didn't merely check off the boxes when it came to water management; they rewrote the playbook. The playbook met the immediate needs for the 2022 Games while also setting a precedent for future events and urban planning. Water scarcity and poor water management are global issues. According to the World Health Organization, more than 785 million people lack a basic drinking-water service. The strategies employed at the Beijing 2022 Winter Olympics have the potential to contribute to global solutions for water management, offering a model that can be adapted to different cultural, economic, and environmental contexts.

The goal of achieving zero waste is ambitious, especially for an event on the scale of the Olympics. However, the Beijing Winter Olympics took this challenge head-on, implementing a comprehensive waste management strategy aimed at minimizing waste and maximizing recycling and composting. Throughout the Olympic venues, composting and recycling stations were strategically placed to encourage waste separation. These weren't just ordinary bins; they were equipped with signage in multiple languages and had QR codes that attendees could scan to educate themselves more about proper waste disposal. The impact of this initiative helped to educate all who were present at the Winter Games. They did this by providing information on how to dispose of waste properly; the stations served to raise awareness about the importance of waste separation. The sorted waste was then processed more efficiently, with organic waste going to composting facilities and recyclables being sent to appropriate recycling centers. This significantly reduced the amount of waste going to landfills.

Confronting the pressing issue of ensuring that people movement was handled in an environmentally sustainable way, the Beijing 2022 Winter Olympics integrated green transportation solutions in every aspect of people and equipment movement throughout the Games, elevating them from optional amenities to essential components of the event's infrastructure. Being fully aware that the transportation sector is a leading source of greenhouse gas emissions worldwide, the Olympic organizers took a proactive approach. They introduced an extensive fleet of electric buses, specifically engineered to transport athletes, officials, and spectators between the various competition venues and the Olympic Village. These electric buses were state-of-the-art, zero-emission vehicles fitted with advanced smart technologies. These technologies served to optimize bus routes in real time, thereby reducing unnecessary mileage and further minimizing the energy required for each journey. This was a clear demonstration of how technology can be leveraged to make even eco-friendly options more efficient. The commitment to green transportation extended well beyond the use of electric buses. The organizers also laid the groundwork for a more sustainable transportation ecosystem, incorporating electric vehicle charging stations strategically placed throughout the Olympic facilities. This not only facilitated the use of electric vehicles but also sent a strong message about the viability of electric transport. Additionally, bike-sharing programs were introduced as an alternative, low-impact mode of transport, encouraging both athletes and spectators to opt for the most energy-efficient travel methods available.

The ramifications of these comprehensive transportation initiatives were multifaceted. On one level, they contributed to a significant reduction in the Games' overall carbon footprint, aligning seamlessly with the broader sustainability objectives set forth by both the International Olympic Committee and global environmental protocols. On another level, the availability of such conscientious transportation choices served as a catalyst for behavioral change among attendees. By experiencing firsthand the efficacy and convenience of these green transportation options, individuals were encouraged to reconsider their typical travel behaviors. This has the potential to inspire long-term changes that could extend well beyond the closing ceremonies, contributing to a more sustainable future on a global scale.

The green initiatives implemented during the Beijing 2022 Winter Olympics were not just symbolic gestures; they had tangible, measurable impacts. From significant reductions in energy consumption thanks to advanced insulation techniques to the successful management of waste through zero-waste initiatives, the Games set new benchmarks in environmental stewardship. The use of electric buses and sustainable infrastructure alone contributed to a marked decrease in the event's carbon footprint, aligning it with global sustainability goals. These are not abstract achievements; they are quantifiable successes that demonstrate the efficacy of marrying sports with sustainability. The Beijing 2022 Winter Olympics serve as a compelling blueprint for future sports events. The meticulous planning and successful execution of various green initiatives have provided a road map that other event organizers can follow. Whether it's the FIFA World Cup, the Super Bowl, or local sporting events, the lessons learned from Beijing offer a scalable and adaptable model. The Games have effectively raised the bar, making it clear that sustainability is achievable on a grand scale. Perhaps the most exciting takeaway is the untapped potential for sports to be a driving force in global sustainability efforts. Sports capture the collective imagination as few other things can. They have the power to unite people across geographical, linguistic, and cultural divides. When this universal appeal is harnessed to promote sustainability, the impact can be monumental. Athletes like Marie-Philip Poulin and Mikaela Shiffrin, who use their platforms to advocate for environmental causes, exemplify how influential sports can be in shaping public opinion and driving change.

As we reflect on the Beijing 2022 Winter Olympics, it's evident that the Games were more than just a showcase of athletic prowess; they demonstrated how sports, technology, and sustainability can come together in a harmonious symphony of progress. The Games have set new standards, not just in athletic achievement but in how we think about the role of large-scale events in our ongoing struggle to build a more sustainable future. They have shown us that with the right mix of innovation, commitment, and public engagement, sports can, indeed, be a catalyst for global change. As the world turns its eyes toward the future, one thing is clear: the intersection of sports, technology, and sustainability is not a passing trend; it's the playing field of the future. And it's a game where everyone stands to win.

ChatGPT and OpenAI
Revolutionizing the World of Sports

In recent months, a transformative force has emerged on the sports scene, reshaping the game's landscape in a manner unparalleled in modern history. This player doesn't wear a jersey, nor does it revel in the thunderous applause of a crowd after a triumphant feat on the field. Its domain is the vast digital cosmos, operating amidst a sea of bits and bytes, yet its ripples reverberate powerfully through the tangible, real world, carving a monumental impact that's hard to overlook. Welcome to the burgeoning era of artificial intelligence (AI), a tidal wave of innovation that's sweeping the sports domain into a new realm of possibilities. At the vanguard of this groundbreaking journey is OpenAI, an organization that's embarking on a daring, ambitious mission to meld the vibrant, effervescent world of sports with the precision and insight of AI, thereby unlocking a boundless galaxy of new possibilities. These are not fanciful notions plucked from a science-fiction tale, but real, imminent shifts on the horizon, poised to redefine the essence of athletic prowess, fan interaction, and the broader ethos that underpins sports culture. The ensuing narrative is not merely about a technological evolution, but a revolutionary fusion that's set to redefine the contours of what's possible in the domain of sports.

OpenAI, as its name suggests, is an open venture into the realm of AI, whose core philosophy hinges on the ethical and responsible development and deployment of artificial general intelligence (AGI). Unlike narrow AI, which is designed and trained for a specific task, AGI carries the promise of outperforming humans at the most economically valuable work, a vision that propels the endeavors at OpenAI. The organization is committed to ensuring that such powerful and transformative technology benefits all of humanity, an ethos that is as profound as it is impactful. The foundation of OpenAI serves as the fertile ground upon which ChatGPT, among other marvels, has been cultivated. ChatGPT is a quintessential representation of OpenAI's mission to bridge the realms of human intuition and machine intelligence. Underpinned by a robust technological framework and fueled by a corpus of diverse data, ChatGPT is a testament to OpenAI's commitment to driving forward the frontier of AI in a manner that is aligned with the broader good of society. As we venture into this new era where AI and sports intersect, the potential for transformative change is immense. The fusion of AI's analytical prowess with the dynamism of sports opens a realm brimming with opportunities. From real-time performance analytics and injury prevention to enriched fan engagement and personalized training regimes, the canvas is wide and the palette is rich, embodying the potential of what AI can bring to the sports arena. Its ability to engage in humanlike conversation, coupled with its analytical acumen, makes it a powerful companion for athletes, coaches, sports analysts, and fans alike.

ChatGPT has quickly become far more than a fleeting trend—it serves as a formidable bridge between the digital realm and the heart of sports. Its capabilities stretch beyond mere data processing, extending into the territory of insightful analysis and synthesis and traversing an expansive ocean of data with the acumen akin to that of a seasoned sports analyst. This tool does not merely skim the surface but delves deep into the data, unearthing insights with a finesse that echoes a human touch yet is powered by machine precision. With every interaction, ChatGPT underscores a new era where AI complements human expertise, embarking on explorations within the sports domain that were once considered beyond reach. Through the lens of ChatGPT, the digital and physical facets of sports converge, unveiling a narrative rich with potential and scripted with the ink of innovation. It's an ally in the sports innovation journey, far outpacing human constraints by processing colossal data volumes at a pace beyond human capability, making it an indispensable companion in the pursuit of sporting excellence. The essence of ChatGPT's prowess lies in its remarkable conversational ability, a trait that propels it far beyond the conventional realm of analytical tools. This extraordinary capability is born from the underlying technology of Generative Pre-trained Transformer 3 (GPT-3), which is the brainchild of OpenAI. The architecture of GPT-3 (and its newer family member, GPT-4) is engineered to comprehend and generate humanlike text, enabling ChatGPT to engage in dialogues that are astonishingly like human interaction. The conversational abilities of ChatGPT are not confined to surface-level engagement; it dives much deeper, fostering a rapport that embodies a sense of understanding and relevance. It's a discourse that is orchestrated with a blend of empathy, relevance, and insight, mirroring the nuances of human communication with uncanny accuracy.

When engaging with athletes, coaches, sports analysts, and fans, ChatGPT navigates through the vast expanses of data at its disposal, extracting and presenting insights in a manner that resonates with human intuition and understanding. This is not about cold, hard facts thrown at users; it's about weaving a narrative that encapsulates the essence of the discussion, providing a context and a perspective that adds a layer of depth to the interaction. When you engage with ChatGPT, the experience is familiar, like you're conversing with a knowledgeable companion, one who not only understands the crux of the matter but also appreciates the emotional and intuitive facets of the conversation. This is particularly impactful in the sports domain, where the emotional quotient is high and the stakes are even higher. Whether it's analyzing a game strategy, evaluating player performance, or simply discussing the dynamics of a recent match, ChatGPT's responses are enriched with a blend of analytical insight and humanlike comprehension. The ability of ChatGPT to engage in meaningful exchanges opens a realm of possibilities for enriched interaction among athletes, coaches, and fans. Imagine a scenario where a fan could have a detailed discussion about a game strategy with a coachlike AI application through the power of ChatGPT, delving into the intricacies of the game, exploring alternative strategies, and gaining insights that were once the domain of seasoned analysts. Similarly, athletes and coaches can engage with ChatGPT to analyze performance data, explore new training regimes, and even devise game strategies. The fluidity of conversation, coupled with the depth of insight, making the interaction immensely valuable and engaging.

The monumental shift ushered in by ChatGPT is the transformation of engagement from a monologue to a dialogue, weaving a fabric of interactive exchange that transcends the conventional boundaries of communication. The responses are tailored based on the flow of the conversation, the queries posed, and the context provided. This dynamic nature of engagement ensures that each interaction is unique, personalized, and insightful. In sports, where every nuance matters, where the thirst for knowledge is insatiable, and the quest for excellence is relentless, ChatGPT has fast become a companion that not only understands the journey but also enriches it with insights that propel toward a horizon of broader understanding and better decision-making.

Imagine a scenario where a soccer club—let's call it "FC Techno"—embraces the capabilities of ChatGPT to enhance its engagement with both its players and its global fan base. On the training ground, FC Techno's coaching staff interacts with ChatGPT to dissect the myriad of player performance metrics collected during training sessions and matches. They pose queries, articulate concerns, and seek advice on strategy formulation. ChatGPT, processing the input and the vast data at its disposal, responds with insightful analysis, suggestions for tactical adjustments, and identification of opponent weaknesses that can be exploited in upcoming matches. The engagement is fluid, contextual, and immensely value-laden, personalizing with each interaction to address the evolving queries and scenarios posed by the coaching staff. In parallel, FC Techno unveils a fan engagement platform powered by ChatGPT. Fans across the globe log in to engage in rich, personalized dialogues about their favorite team. They inquire about player statistics, upcoming match strategies, and even historical performance analyses. ChatGPT navigates through each query, providing detailed responses, sharing intriguing insights, and even offering interactive visual representations of player and team performances. Fans are no longer lean-back recipients of static information; they're active participants, leaning into a dynamic, interactive dialogue that satiates their curiosity, fuels their passion, and strengthens their bond with FC Techno. Each fan's experience on the platform is unique, molded by their individual interactions and the evolving dialogue they share with ChatGPT. As the season progresses, the iterative dialogue between FC Techno's coaching staff and ChatGPT refines the team's strategies, contributing to a remarkable upturn in their performance on the field. The narrative of FC Techno's triumphant season is not solely a tale of human athleticism and coaching brilliance; it's also a testament to the enriched engagement fostered by ChatGPT. Similarly, the enriched dialogue on the fan engagement platform fosters a thriving community of ardent supporters whose bond with the club is now deeper, more insightful, and engaging. Through this lens, the scenario vividly illustrates how ChatGPT transforms the paradigm of engagement from a mere monologue to a rich, insightful dialogue, seamlessly intertwining with the realm of sports to foster a culture of continuous learning, exploration, and shared passion, both on and off the field.

The frontier of sports technology is being continually expanded through synergistic collaborations and partnerships. When stalwarts from the domain of AI, like OpenAI, join forces with entities steeped in sporting tradition and expertise, the potential for groundbreaking innovation is immense. For example, when developers at a prestigious football league develop AI-driven solutions aimed at enhancing player performance analysis, fan engagement, and real-time game analytics, it could also yield a platform where coaches and analysts can interact with ChatGPT to delve deeper into player statistics. This would enable them to identify tactical nuances and even predict opponent strategies based on historical data. This partnership between OpenAI and the football league has the beginnings of a new era in data-driven coaching, where AI becomes a quintessential part of the strategic arsenal, aiding in the meticulous preparation for games and the holistic development of athletes. The real-time insights generated could significantly augment the decision-making process during live games, providing a tactical edge in a highly competitive environment. Similarly, a partnership between OpenAI and a global sports broadcasting network to enhance the real-time analysis and commentary during live sports events. ChatGPT, with its ability to process vast amounts of data in real time and generate humanlike text, can provide a layer of insightful analysis, enriching the commentary with statistical nuances and historical context that adds depth to the viewing experience at a pace not previously achievable with in-place technology. On the broadcasting frontier, the work these companies are doing together is redefining the narrative of live sports commentary. The AI-powered analysis would not only educate the viewers but also enrich the narrative with a depth of analysis that caters to both the casual viewer and the sports aficionado.

The ripple effects of such collaborations extend beyond the immediate realm of sports. The technological advancements fostered through these partnerships contribute to the broader domain of AI and machine learning, propelling the capabilities of systems like ChatGPT to new heights. This then increases the scope and pace of cross-pollination of ideas; expertise could spawn innovations that transcend the sporting arena, finding applications in myriad other domains. The relationship between sports and AI, exemplified through the collaborations with OpenAI, captures a promise of a future where the essence of human endeavor is celebrated, analyzed, and elevated through the lens of cutting-edge technology.

The potential for innovation at this intersection heralds a horizon that is full of endless possibilities, not only within the sports domain but across the vast expanse of societal and industrial landscapes.

The rapid advancement of AI in sports marks a new phase of innovation, bringing together athletic ability and machine intelligence to create new levels of achievement. However, like any significant technological development, the intersection of AI and sports brings about a set of ethical dilemmas. There are a range of ethical factors to consider, spanning issues such as maintaining fairness in sports, ensuring data privacy, and preserving the essence of human effort and achievement in athletic competition. These considerations present a complex scenario where the benefits of AI need to be balanced against the principles that form the foundation of sports and the rights of individuals involved.

Sportsmanship is fundamentally built on the principles of fair competition, integrity, and human effort. The introduction of AI technologies like ChatGPT, which have the capability to analyze and predict outcomes based on historical data, presents new challenges and uncertainties in the sports sector. A critical ethical concern is the potential of AI to disrupt the level playing field. For example, wealthier teams might leverage advanced AI tools to secure an unfair advantage in player recruitment, performance optimization, or game strategy formulation. This could potentially widen the gap between well-resourced teams and those with fewer resources, challenging the core principle of fair competition that is central to sports. Additionally, the use of AI in sports brings up valid questions about data privacy and consent. A significant amount of data is collected from athletes, including performance metrics and biometric data, which can be analyzed extensively using AI. The collection, storage, and analysis of such sensitive data raises potential concerns regarding privacy, consent, and data security. Key questions around who owns this data, who can access it, and for what purposes it can be used are central to the ethical application of AI in sports. Addressing these ethical challenges requires a deep understanding of the potential issues and a proactive approach to developing solutions that adhere to the principles of fairness, transparency, and respect for individual rights.

One major challenge is the potential worsening of inequalities both within and between sports entities due to the deployment of AI. A potential solution could involve the establishment of regulatory frameworks and governing bodies specifically dedicated to overseeing the ethical use of AI in sports. These bodies could work toward ensuring fair access to AI technologies, thereby promoting a level playing field. The issues of data privacy and consent call for strong legal frameworks that clearly outline the rights and responsibilities of all stakeholders involved, ranging from sports entities and athletes to AI developers like OpenAI. Clear guidelines on data ownership, consent protocols, and privacy safeguards are crucial for building a culture of trust and ethical compliance. Promoting a culture of transparency and open discussion among all stakeholders can significantly aid in navigating the ethical landscape. This inclusive approach fosters a collaborative environment where different perspectives can be shared and understood, paving the way for well-informed decisions. Moreover, it cultivates a sense of collective responsibility toward addressing the ethical implications of AI in sports, ensuring that the technology is employed in a manner that aligns with the core values of fairness and integrity inherent in athletics. An open dialogue can also serve as a platform for educating all involved parties on the potential benefits and challenges posed by AI, thus promoting a more nuanced understanding of the technology and its impact on the sports sector. Furthermore, transparency and open discourse can contribute to building trust, a crucial element in ensuring the successful integration of AI in sports, while adhering to ethical guidelines. Through these discussions, a consensus on best practices and regulatory frameworks can be forged, which in turn will help in setting a standard for how AI technologies like ChatGPT are deployed in the sports industry in an ethical and beneficial manner. Engaging athletes, teams, fans, and tech entities in a dialogue about the ethical implications of AI in sports, and collaboratively working toward crafting solutions, is a key step toward ensuring that the intersection of AI and sports happens in a way that upholds the fundamental principles of sportsmanship and ethical integrity. This open dialogue could help in addressing concerns, understanding different perspectives, and working toward a common goal of ensuring ethical adherence while advancing the application of AI in the sports domain.

Despite the concerns outlined, the potential of AI and ChatGPT in sports is undeniably vast and holds a promise of significantly enhancing many aspects of the sports industry. The collaboration between sports entities and AI developers can foster innovation, driving the development of new tools and applications tailored to meet the unique needs of the sports sector. This collaborative innovation can potentially lead to the creation of new standards and best practices that address ethical concerns, ensuring that the deployment of AI in sports is done responsibly and beneficially. The journey of integrating AI and ChatGPT in sports, though laden with ethical considerations, is a pathway that, navigated wisely, can lead to a new era of sports where technology augments human endeavor, enriches fan engagement, and contributes to a deeper appreciation of the athletic prowess on display. Through proactive engagement on ethical considerations, clear regulatory frameworks, and a commitment to transparency and open dialogue, the sports industry can harness the power of AI to usher in a new era of athletic excellence and fan engagement.

The synergy between ChatGPT and the sports domain is poised for a significant evolution in the coming years. Given the current trajectory of technological advancements and the growing acceptance of AI applications in sports, it's reasonable to predict that OpenAI and ChatGPT will play a substantial role in changing how teams train, strategize, and engage with fans. Its ability to analyze vast amounts of data rapidly makes it a powerful tool for sports analytics. Teams and athletes could leverage this capability to gain deeper insights into performance metrics, enabling more informed decisions on training and strategy. This is already leading to a higher level of competition as teams become more adept at utilizing the insights gleaned from AI analysis. Fan engagement is an area that is exploding with growth thanks to ChatGPT. As fans crave more interactive and insightful experiences, the personalized and real-time engagement facilitated by ChatGPT significantly enhances the way fans interact with their favorite teams and athletes. This goes beyond one-size-fits-all engagement; it's about building stronger relationships between sports entities and their fans, enriching the overall sports culture based on how each fan interacts with their favorite sports teams.

In terms of further integration and innovation, the future looks bright! The collaborative efforts between AI developers and sports entities could lead to the development of new, tailored AI applications that address the unique needs and challenges of the sports sector. The sports industry has always been a fertile ground for technological innovation, and with the advent of AI technologies like ChatGPT, the pace of innovation is set to accelerate further. There's a potential for a paradigm shift, where the conventional boundaries between athletes, coaches, fans, and technology become more fluid, fostering a more integrated and enriched sports ecosystem. One of the significant areas of collaboration is the development of wearable technology integrated with AI for real-time performance monitoring. Imagine smart wearables equipped with sensors powered by ChatGPT, capable of providing real-time feedback to athletes and coaches during training sessions and competitions. This real-time data analysis and feedback could enable athletes to optimize their performance dynamically while coaches could make informed decisions on strategies based on live data. Enhanced virtual reality (VR) experiences for fans is another frontier. The integration of ChatGPT with VR technology could lead to highly immersive fan experiences, where fans could virtually experience the game from the field, interact with players, or even participate in virtual sports events. These VR experiences, powered by AI, could provide fans with unprecedented access to the game, creating a new level of engagement and loyalty.

This wave of innovation extends to advanced analytics platforms for assisting in the setting of complex game strategies. With ChatGPT's ability to sift through vast data sets and derive meaningful insights, the creation of advanced analytics platforms could revolutionize game strategy formulation. Teams could have access to comprehensive analytics dashboards, providing a holistic view of both their performance and that of their competitors, enabling more sophisticated and data-driven strategies. Powered by AI, the potential for creating personalized fan experiences is immense. ChatGPT could power platforms that provide fans with personalized content, interactive platforms, and real-time game insights, significantly enhancing fan engagement. In a digital age where personalization is key, the ability to provide fans with tailored experiences could set sports entities apart in a crowded marketplace. Beyond fan engagement and athlete performance, ChatGPT also has a large role to play a role in talent scouting and recruitment. AI-powered analytics is significantly streamlining the process of identifying and recruiting new talent, ensuring that teams have the best possible roster. By analyzing historical performance data, social media, and other publicly available data, ChatGPT could help teams identify promising talent efficiently. Thinking bigger, the realm of sports medicine could also benefit from the integration of AI. ChatGPT, with its data analysis capabilities, could assist in injury prevention, rehabilitation, and the overall well-being of athletes. By analyzing historical injury data, biomechanical data, and other relevant metrics, ChatGPT could help sports medical professionals in diagnosing, treating, and preventing injuries. The potential applications of ChatGPT in sports are vast, and the collaborative efforts between AI developers and sports entities could spawn a new era of innovation addressing the unique needs and challenges of the sports sector. As these collaborative efforts mature, the sports industry could witness the emergence of new technologies and platforms that redefine the landscape of sports analytics, fan engagement, and athlete performance.

The scope for innovation also extends to addressing the ethical concerns associated with AI in sports. The development of robust frameworks for data privacy, consent, and equitable access to AI technology could be part of the innovation agenda. Through proactive regulation and the establishment of clear ethical guidelines, the sports industry can ensure that the integration of AI technologies like ChatGPT is done in a responsible and beneficial manner. The potential of ChatGPT's integration into a vast array of sports is undeniable, indicating a wide avenue for additional integration and innovation that could significantly alter many elements of the sports ecosystem. As the sports sector progressively acknowledges the potential of AI, the function of ChatGPT, along with other similar AI technologies, is projected to become increasingly central in propelling the narrative of sports into a new epoch characterized by technological augmentation.

ChatGPT acts as a digital companion in the relentless pursuit of sporting excellence. It serves as a facilitator of meaningful dialogues between athletes, coaches, fans, and stakeholders. It's not just a tool but a catalyst for ushering in a new era of enriched and insightful interaction within the sports domain. Through this unique blend of humanlike interaction and data-driven insight, ChatGPT is essentially redefining the parameters of what's feasible at the intersection of sports and technology. The core advantage of ChatGPT lies in its ability to process vast expanses of data, churn out meaningful insights, and engage in interactive dialogues. This trifecta of capabilities makes it an asset in a myriad of sports-related applications, be it in coaching, performance analysis, fan engagement, or even sports journalism. The opportunities for further integration are vast, ranging from real-time analysis during games to fostering deeper connections between teams and their fan base. The innovative potential extends beyond ChatGPT to other AI technologies, each carving out its niche of influence within the sports sector. Whether through performance optimization, enhancing fan experiences, or streamlining operational efficiencies, AI is poised to become a cornerstone in the modern sports landscape.

As the evolution of AI technologies like ChatGPT continues, so does the breadth of opportunities for further integration and innovation within sports. The trajectory is aimed toward a future where the synergy between ChatGPT and sports is not just a novelty but an integral component of the sporting ecosystem. The fusion of AI with sports is opening doors to unexplored avenues, each holding the promise of elevating the sports domain to new pinnacles of excellence, engagement, and insight. The continuous development and refinement of ChatGPT, coupled with its growing adoption within the sports community, are strong indicators of the transformative journey that lies ahead. The narrative of sports stands on the brink of a transformative epoch with ChatGPT and its AI stablemates are poised to usher in a realm of boundless possibilities, heralding a new chapter where the once-rigid boundaries of what's conceivable are relentlessly redrawn.

Acknowledgments

The journey of writing this, my first book, was a profound exploration, and like any venture into the unknown, it was both challenging and exhilarating. It would not have been possible without the support, encouragement, and collaboration of many individuals to whom I am deeply grateful.

First and foremost, I extend my heartfelt gratitude to my family, Bernadette, Sadie, and Avery. Without your unwavering belief in my capabilities, this simply would not have been possible. I am immensely thankful to the John Wiley & Sons team. Thank you to my editor, Elizabeth Kuball; your keen eye and thoughtful feedback were indispensable in shaping the narrative. A massive thank-you to Satish Gowrishankar and Magesh Elangovan; your patience and professionalism have left an indelible mark on every page.

I am also grateful to my colleagues in the sports technology community, whose pioneering work provided both the inspiration and the foundation upon which this book is built. Special thanks to my colleagues, Susanne Tedrick and Jake Switzer, two of the greatest teammates I have had the pleasure of suiting up with. Thank you to the many customers I have had the pleasure to work with over the years and the awesome heroes on the field of play that sparked my undying love for sport. A shout-out to the South African rugby team, past and present, whose camaraderie and passion for the game have always reminded me of the pure joy that sports bring into our lives.

Lastly, I want to express my gratitude to you, the readers, who have embarked on this exploration with me. Your engagement and feedback are not only rewarding but also provide the motivation for continuous learning and sharing.

This book is a testament to the fact that learning and discovery are collaborative endeavors. I am honored to share this journey with all of you.

About the Author

From the rugby fields to the pristine waves of South Africa, Jon Flynn's love for sports was kindled at a tender age. It was here that he cultivated a profound appreciation for the boundless potential that existed in the synergy between human endeavor and the forces of nature. This early passion set the stage for a lifelong journey that would see Jon traverse the thrilling juncture of sports and technology.

As an award-winning sports technologist, Jon seamlessly marries the vibrant realm of sports with the meticulous precision of data analytics and artificial intelligence (AI). His mastery of data-driven strategies has been a beacon, guiding numerous initiatives aimed at harnessing real-time insights to empower athletes and teams in optimizing their performance. Venturing into the domain of AI, Jon has pioneered ground-breaking applications that have significantly enriched performance analysis and fan engagement. His innovative exploits have extended to crafting immersive sporting experiences that resonate with enthusiasts on a profound level.

Beyond the tangible realm, Jon's adept utilization of generative AI has created engaging narratives that delve into the heart of athletic competition and strategy, embodying the essence of sportsmanship in a digital narrative. His eloquence extends to the stage as a sought-after keynote speaker, where he passionately discusses the burgeoning convergence of sports and technology. His words not only spark lively discussions but inspire a collective ambition to explore the uncharted territories where athleticism meets machine intelligence.

Jon's extensive contributions to the sports technology spectrum continue to propel the industry into a new epoch of technological augmentation. His endeavors encapsulate the boundless potential nestled at the intersection of sports and AI, forging a path for others to explore and innovate and continuing the narrative that intertwines the primal essence of sports with the evolving frontier of technological innovation.

Index